RICHARD MULVANEY.

CHASING THE STORY GOD

CHASING the STORY GOD

Mike McCardell

HARBOUR PUBLISHING

Harbour Publishing
P.O. Box 219
Madeira Park, BC
Canada V0N 2H0

THE CANADA COUNCIL | LE CONSEIL DES ARTS
FOR THE ARTS | DU CANADA
SINCE 1957 | DEPUIS 1957

We acknowledge the financial support of the Government of Canada through the
Book Publishing Industry Development Program for our publishing activities.
We further acknowledge the support of the Canada Council for the Arts and the
Province of British Columbia through the British Columbia Arts Council for our
publishing program.

Printed in Canada.

Author photograph by David Ingram.
Cover design by Martin Nichols.

This book was printed using vegetable-based inks on acid-free paper containing
100% recycled, post-consumer fibre and was processed without using chlorine.
This 100% old-growth-free paper was provided by New Leaf Papers.

National Library of Canada Cataloguing in Publication Data

McCardell, Mike, 1944–
  Chasing the story god

ISBN 1-55017-248-4

1. McCardell, Mike, 1944– 2. Television journalists—British Columbia—
Vancouver—Biography. 3. Vancouver (B.C.)—Anecdotes. I. Title.
PN4913.M36A3 2001   070'.92   C2001-910906-7

To Valerie

Contents

# Preface

The last story on the News Hour on BCTV in Vancouver is about some ordinary event, like a girl jumping in a puddle or a boy digging up a worm. I am lucky enough to do those stories, although both the boss and my wife would rather that I was doing hard news because both of them believe that the meat and bones of news shows are real, tough-nosed events.

My wife laments the day I stopped chasing police cars. That is the nitty gritty of life, she says. I met her when I was a crime reporter and took her along on some stories where the sky was red with swirling police lights and the sound of sirens replaced the jukebox music that most girls were listening to on dates. She got to know me that way, and we were married. Now she says, "You are not doing another story on flowers, are you? You are just trying to get out of real work."

Well, as with all things she is right, because hanging

around kids with water pistols cannot be considered an over-ly burdensome way to earn a living, while doing the same thing with adults with real guns is very serious work. Plus stories about kite flying and butterflies simply make me feel good, which is a wonderful fringe benefit.

And since I started doing these stories, the question I hear most often is how do I find them? In fact, how does any-one find a shoe in the middle of the street, or a little boy who is missing pre-school because he has a broken leg and now wants to be a doctor, or an abandoned goldfish in a forgot-ten pond? The secret: despite all the advice given by jour-nalism schools, they come by luck. They come when you turn a corner. They come by talking to people. They come because a cameraman says get out of the van you lazy boob and talk to someone.

And most of all, they come after a lifetime of looking through the eyes of a kid who got hooked on the magical world inside newspapers and wanted to hang out with the characters who make up the stories of everyday life. I put the two together and had a job.

This book describes what you should learn in reporting school: how to find this kind of story, how to find any kind of story—in fact, how to find almost anything in life. What you basically do is walk out your front door, look around at what is in front of you and say, "Wow!"

Acknowledgements

I have done seven thousand stories for television. I have forty pounds of newspaper clippings and a box of magazine articles. Almost every one of those stories has allowed me to meet people who have helped me in my life. Almost every person I have written about has taught me something. Sometimes it is a bitter lesson, and sometimes they are profiles in courage.

To every person I have ever written about, thank you. You have given me the inspiration to get up each morning and look for one more of you who is ordinary on the outside and extraordinary in your heart and in your spirit.

I would also like to thank Mike Steele, a newspaper editor, who hired me to write a column some years ago, which he suggested should be turned into a book.

That, of course, was too easy. So this book came out of the typewriter.

11

The book that he suggested is still to come, so he will get thanked twice.

And I want to thank Mary Schendlinger, an editor, whom I met after the manuscript for this was written but before it became a book. When she holds a pencil it becomes a magic wand, and she made lazy sentences in here stand up and dance. Chilly would have said she is very good. In a while you will learn what that means.

A Basic Education:
Part I

I was very lucky. My career sort of came to me as a gift and it saved me from having to dig ditches for a living. I am not saying digging ditches is bad—it is better exercise than typing, and if you are working for the government the pay is probably better—but journalism is a lot of fun. I will tell you how it all happened.

I did not do well in school. I was always looking out the window wondering if those clouds in the sky were going to crash into each other. Somehow the teachers knew when I was playing cloud traffic controller because that was when they called on me and asked where the preposition was in the sentence they had just read. I was not as good with prepositions as I was with clouds.

Then I was kept in school after three o'clock along with the other kids who forgot their homework or who didn't know where the preposition was or who were caught punching each other in the nose. Sometimes I was serving time for all three offences. In addition there was morning detention for those who had no afternoons left to be punished in before the end of the school year. And there was dry lunch for those who had no mornings or afternoons left for punishment. For a while I went in early, then ate lunch with no water to wash down a sandwich, then stayed in after three o'clock. I didn't really like school.

But in these detentions, all of which were served in silence, I noticed that the poor teachers who were assigned to sit in front of the class of misfits always did the same thing. They read the *Daily News*.

The *Daily News* was New York's tabloid newspaper. Like all tabloids, its stories were short and they were basically about crime, corruption and oddball people, and there were plenty of comics. Low-class people supposedly read the *Daily News*. High-class people, such as teachers, were supposed to read the *New York Times*.

The teachers all came to work carrying the *Times*, or the *Wall Street Journal*. But in the folds of those papers they carried the *Daily News* and the *New York Post*. The *Times* had long articles on politics and economics but never, never any comics.

Hence, during the years I was going to school, the *New York Times* sold about 600,000 copies a day around the world. The *Daily News* sold 1.5 million copies a day, and on Sundays, when they said the heck with news and put the comics on page one, they sold 2.5 million. Somehow, I think, a lesson was to be learned: serious news is important, but tales of ordinary folks and a good laugh sell better.

Anyway, while I was sitting in detention I started reading the *Daily News* and I was fascinated by stories of criminals with names like Two Finger Maloney and crime bosses who had more power than the mayor without having to worry about votes. There was a story about an idiot who tried to sail a homemade raft across the East River just for the fun of it, and a couple going on their honeymoon around the world on a Harley. In fact there were endless stories about ordinary people whose lives would make you laugh or cry or scratch your head.

Those were people I liked, and I wondered what could be better than spending a lifetime with them. So, very simply, I decided to be a reporter. That was all there was to it. The fact that I still didn't know where the preposition was didn't matter; I wanted to be with the kind of people who got in the *Daily News*.

For two years during high school I lived in Germany. This came about purely as a fluke and is explained later, but while I was there I got to see and meet more off-the-page characters than anyone could ever invent. Among the row after row of bombed-out buildings there were spies and saboteurs—one of whom tried to kill my mother, among other people—and counterspies, one of whom saved her. And there were friends I made who faced tanks and crawled under barbed wire to escape from communism. By the time they were teenagers they had lived five lifetimes, and I was lucky enough to spend a few years growing up with them.

I was sixteen when I returned to New York and went to work in the local taxicab garage. Every kid in my neighbourhood worked in the taxi garage from the day they were legally able to at sixteen until the day they graduated from high school when they got a real job.

We worked after school, all day on Saturday and three hours on Sunday. We pumped gas into the lines of cabs that came in between shifts. We checked the hot radiator of every cab by putting a big cloth over the cap and leaning on it and turning it and saying, "God, please don't let the steam blow up." And when the last cab was in, we swept out the mammoth dirty garage. Then we went home for dinner.

We had every other Sunday off. And like all the kids of my entire generation, we gave half our pay to our mothers, who put it toward the rent.

In that garage was Tiny, the toothless, friendly three hundred-pound mechanic who could lift a six-cylinder engine out of a car, but who was afraid of Mo, the cigar-smoking dispatcher who screamed at everyone, especially us if we dribbled gasoline: "I'll take that out of your pay!" I learned I didn't like people who scream.

Then the day finally came when I graduated from high school, half a year later than I should have. Prepositions can hold you back. And to celebrate, my mother bought a six-pack of beer and two sandwiches of ham on rye.

My mother had raised me by herself. She left my father, who was an alcoholic and fairly brutal, when I was in grade two. I remember the morning before sunrise that she woke me up and said, "Be quiet and follow me." We tiptoed out of the house and from that moment on she was a single work-ing parent, in an age when women always got paid less than men. We ate hot dogs for dinner a great deal. She was a brave woman.

"What do you want to do now?" she asked.

"I want to be a reporter."

Her solution was simple. "Go to a newspaper," she said. And to make sure I went, she gave me a subway token.

The train stopped at Times Square. I went up into the *New York Times* office. My mother would be proud, I thought. They offered me a job as an outdoor messenger.

I walked across town to the *Daily News*. They offered me a job as an indoor messenger. It was winter. Winter in New York is cold. I took the indoor job, and stayed at the *Daily News* for eleven years.

The day after I got the job I promised to paint my moth-er's apartment. Halfway through it I went out into the snowy streets to get some air. That was an act of bad timing. Neighbourhoods then were like separate warring countries and kids from each neighbourhood protected their territory like pit bulls, for no reason other than they had nothing else to do.

A few days earlier a fellow from another neighbourhood had been in a fight with someone from my neighbourhood and he had lost. To get revenge on us, the other neighbour-hood's kids were out looking for someone from my neigh-bourhood. Into this lack of mutual understanding I mistakenly went out to clear the paint from my lungs.

I walked over the soot-covered snow that was piled in

drifts alongside parked cars. The air felt good, the cold felt good, then I saw the fellows from the other neighbourhood coming down a street toward me and I realized I was more than two blocks from home. That was alien territory. I turned around, but more of them were coming from that way too. I ran down a side street but they caught me, and while several of them held my arms, one of them, as the court document later read, "did take clenched fist and repeatedly strike the complainant on and about the face."

They left me bleeding in the snow with a hole where my tooth was. My mother was not pleased when I returned home, and she called the police because one person could fight another, but group trouncing was frowned upon.

I was not pleased either because I had to go to the dentist now instead of starting my career in journalism. He drilled down a good tooth and put a temporary piece of plastic on it and told me to duck next time. The next day I went to work in the *Daily News* mailroom, seven floors below the newsroom, surrounded by other eighteen- and nineteen-year-olds who looked about as well educated as I did.

I went to lunch with them in a locker room and took out my sandwich. I bit into it, and after I chewed through the ham and cheese the temporary crown on my tooth got stuck in the rye bread and came off in my mouth. Damn. I couldn't open my mouth and say I had my tooth in there mixed up with the half-mushed bread. Not on my first day. I couldn't stick my fingers in my mouth and pull out my tooth; that's not the way you start off new friendships. I couldn't chew because I was afraid I was going to break the little sliver of real tooth that the crown was stuck on. And I didn't know where the toilet was and I couldn't open my mouth and ask.

So I sat there, not chewing, waiting for them to go back to work. I knew they thought I was wacko, but there are so many odd people in the world it didn't matter. Eventually they left and I fixed my tooth. There was a lesson in that: with temporary crowns, don't eat hard bread.

Over the next handful of years I did what many young fellows did. I went to work, got my teeth fixed, met a pretty girl and got married. I worked my way slowly out of the mail-room and into the newsroom as a copy boy on the night shift, where the duties were to change typewriter ribbons, sharpen pencils and, much more important, get beer after the bars had closed at night.

This was in an age when people drank in newsrooms. There was the popular image of the hard-drinking, two-fist-ed reporter, and the more you drank the more you thought you fit that image. There were no objections to drinking on the job so long as your writing was tight and your spelling was good. And since no one could spell worth a damn if they drank too much, no one—except those who would eventual-ly be fired—drank too much.

This was also part of the training of those who wanted to be reporters. Knowing the subjects you are writing about and the places they live in are the most important things in reporting. In fact, they are the only things. And to learn this, copy boys were sent out with reporters and photographers to do menial tasks like carrying film from disaster scenes back to the newspaper office.

But you had to carry it faster than a taxicab. Anyone could pop the film into a cab, but a good copy boy would use a variety of back streets, subways and rides bummed on garbage trucks to deliver the film while the taxi was still stuck in traffic. The goal of the editors was to get the film fast, along with training young people who knew how to get around in the city.

Beer was important because you could not be a reporter unless you knew how to get beer at three a.m., an hour after the bars closed. It was a very important test given to all the copy boys, and girls, and that is probably why it was assigned so often. Reporters who learn to work only with press releases are not real reporters. Reporters who deal only with legitimate authority figures are not real reporters. Copy boys and girls who can get beer at three a.m. have some potential.

I spent countless nights getting beer, and hanging around police stations and outside burning buildings. By the time I was twenty I thought the entire world was made up of crooks and firemen and taxi drivers and illegal beer merchants. And I learned the most important thing in the world was listening to them, and then trying to retell their stories just as they told them.

Time passed. I became a reporter and almost immediately the US government decided to congratulate me with a draft notice.

How I Helped Save the Western World

It was more than thirty-five years ago that I was part of a small band of warriors that held back the communist hordes and kept the world safe for democracy. I also learned the military necessity of golf.

My understanding of military strategy began when I finished basic training in the US Air Force and they gave me the heaviest overcoat I had ever seen. It weighed thirty pounds and would keep me warm in minus-40 degree winds. Then they sent me to a base in Florida.

The mission of the base was to blow Cuba out of existence on a moment's notice. This was just after the Cuban Missile Crisis and Cuba and America were like two cowboys facing each other in the street, spitting and snarling, each waiting for the other to draw first. Every Air Force and Navy base from Florida to Texas had enough ships and airplanes to sink the island, which may be one reason why Castro had a very poor opinion of America.

I told the Air Force that I was a reporter so they assigned me to a civil engineering squadron. Okay, I thought, I will be building bridges or runways, and that might be as exciting as reporting. My speciality, my orders said, was entomology.

"What's that?" I asked my friendly basic training sergeant.

He said he didn't know big words, but I would be serving a greater cause, whatever it was.

Entomology, I learned, is the study of insects. But to the Air Force that meant only one thing: killing them. Killing them in mass numbers, killing them without considering nature's plans.

"The Air Force is not in the business of backing down," my sergeant in the pest control unit said. "If we are ordered to kill them, we kill them."

The insects that were most annoying at this base were the mosquitoes on the officers' golf course. The colonels and generals hated having their games disrupted by buzzing. Before spending a day in mock battles they liked to get in at least nine holes so they could feel they had accomplished something significant.

"We move out tomorrow at 0600," said the sergeant, who had made a career out of attacking mosquitoes. "The golf course opens at 8:00, and we want those bugs dead."

At daybreak on my first morning of battle I was in the back of a blue Air Force pickup truck. It was packed with barrels of powdered DDT and one large gasoline-powered blower that had a cannon-sized barrel for blasting out the dust. My mission was to dump the poison into the top of the blower, fire up the motor and employ chemical warfare from the first to the eighteenth hole.

I could see my sergeant's face in the rear-view mirror and I knew I was looking at the zealous countenance of a warrior. "Fire!" he shouted as he pushed the truck into first gear.

I dumped a barrel of DDT into the blower and blasted it out the cannon. It was too noisy to hear myself shout and the dust swirled around so fast that the battlefield disappeared in a cloud of blowing white powder. The sergeant stuck his fist out the window and raised his thumb. We were attacking.

I dumped and blasted and dumped and blasted. I had to squint to see, but all I could make out were my fingers gripping the blower. They were coated thick with DDT. I tried to breathe through my teeth to strain out the dust that covered me from my Air Force cap to my Air Force boots.

When we stopped to reload, my friendly new sergeant told me, "Don't worry, this stuff only kills mosquitoes. It won't hurt you." The Air Force had told him that and the Air Force would never lie, he said. And the Air Force had taught us always to believe our sergeants because they had shown superior intelligence by staying in the Air Force.

This sergeant really wanted to be a fighter pilot, but that would have meant fitting into a cockpit, which he plainly could not. So he pretended he was flying as he drove over the golf course. He would attack the ninth hole with his foot to the floor and the afterburners in his mind's eye glowing red-hot. Then he would bank sharply to the left and go after those commie mosquitoes on the thirteenth hole.

All the while I held onto the back of the truck trying to empty barrels of DDT down into the blower, bombing those enemy bugs with 500 pounds of white explosives on every mission. Until, that is, the day the sergeant hit a small hill near the fifth hole so fast that the whole truck went airborne. A pilot at last, he had achieved flight. But in the back of the truck the blower also achieved flight—and my foot slipped under it just as it came down.

When the dust cleared, I had earned five broken toes defending the golf course. For a while I was put on light duty, crawling under barracks looking for termites. But as soon as my wounds healed, I was back on the front lines, the tail gunner on the sergeant's four-wheeled mosquito bomber.

I have no doubt, in my own heart, that I saved uncountable golf games, and therefore probably saved the world, because you know you can't win a war if your generals are scratching bites instead of plotting battles.

Now I don't even use weed and feed on my grass, but I still cannot pass a golf course without shouting "Bombs away!" and wondering what to do with that overcoat, which still hangs in my closet.

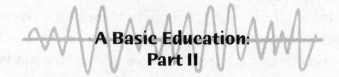

A Basic Education:
Part II

After the Air Force I went back to school. Luckily the US government was paying for a little over half of my college education, which is what it does after you serve in the military. And the *Daily News* was paying for a little over half of it too, because they now wanted their employees to be as smart as those at the *New York Times*. As a result I was making a profit by going to school, which is a very educational thing to do.

Sometimes I did my homework sitting on hard benches in old-fashioned police stations as people in handcuffs passed in front of me. Sometimes I did my studying with the books propped up on a manual typewriter after midnight in a city room with lights that never went out and surrounded by reporters and editors, many of them still drinking beer and shouting about fires and deaths and scandals. It was always after midnight because most crime took place at night and so that's when most crime reporters worked. And one night I was doing my studying while sitting on a curb outside of a rioting prison.

It was October 3, 1970. In front of me police cars lined the street and on the other side of them was a prison that had flames and smoke coming from some of its barred windows. No one was doing anything to put out the fires.

Six of the prisons inside the city had been rioting for nearly a week. It was easy to understand why. The jails were crowded, and they were not filled with nice people to begin with. There were two prisoners in cells designed for one. There were three where two should be. The result was hostility, not only against the system but also against each other and against the walls and sinks and toilets and beds. This was a year before the inmates at Attica, a state prison in New York, rioted and forty-three people were killed by gunfire.

In New York City the rioting began when inmates grabbed some guards and then started ripping up their cells. News spread to the other prisons and within two days there was an explosion of vengeance and violence in one old greybrick prison building after the next. Shredded mattresses were set on fire and pushed out between the bars to the sidewalks below. A block away you could hear screams from inside. In all, twenty-six hostages were taken.

Still, the life of the city went on. Commuters still poured by on their way to work while the hostages lived in terror and the inmates shouted through the slotted-barred windows and the police were paid overtime while waiting for something to happen.

On the first night of the rioting I was sent to a prison in the borough of Queens. The ten storey-high, two block-long prison has a courthouse below it. The last time I had been there was when the fellow who did the punching on my face went to jail.

Now, eight years later, back outside the jail where my attacker served his ninety days, I was watching prisoners smash through the heavy opaque-glass building blocks that made up one of the upper-floor walls. A minister who was rooting for the inmates told me and several other reporters that they "were just trying to see heaven." I quoted him in a story, but I suspected that what they were seeking was more of an earthly view and visitation.

Prison riots, like most major events, quickly settle into a routine. After the initial explosion everything becomes a time-numbing wait for something else to happen, but no one knows whose turn it is to move.

By the third night of the siege the prison I was assigned to was deathly quiet. Floodlights were trained on the exits of the building and police stood in the shadows. There were no negotiations going on, and there was concern for the hostages, who had not been seen since the first day. But nothing was expected to happen that night. No movement was visible inside the prison and police and reporters and onlookers stood around in small groups drinking coffee from Styrofoam cups.

I sat under a street light reading my textbook and

doing my homework. I hoped to study until the sun rose. At three a.m. two policemen, one of them a sergeant, came to where I was sitting. Several other reporters were nearby.

"You want to go inside?" the sergeant asked.

"What do you mean 'inside'?" I asked.

"Inside the prison. Where do you think I mean 'inside'?"

He was not in a good mood.

"The inmates want to talk to some reporters. They want to show the hostages are alive."

Opportunity was beating on my head.

"I'll go!"

"They want a photographer, too."

The photographer I was working with that night was Frank Giorandino, the son of an Italian immigrant, who had been covering crime stories for ten years and was more cautious than I was. He did not think going into the prison was such a good idea.

"We could wind up as hostages."

"Great," I said. "Can you picture the story we'll get?"

"Can you picture us dead?"

"If you go, we take no responsibility," the sergeant said.

Five of us reluctantly volunteered, including Frank. Prison officials said all they could do was cross their fingers. "If anything goes wrong there's no way we can help."

I had another concern. I was going on vacation the following week. We weren't going away, we didn't have enough money for that, but at least for a week I would only go to school and then sleep at night. My concern was that I had been given my vacation pay—in cash, as they did then—along with my regular week's pay as soon as I had arrived at work. Now I was standing with $300 in my pocket in front of a prison filled with men who had a bad habit of taking things that didn't belong to them.

"Be careful, and good luck," the sergeant said.

The police opened a heavy, black steel door and we walked into a dimly lit and very cold concrete tunnel. The door closed behind us. If you ever want to know how much fear you can tolerate, that's a good way to test it. I could taste the adrenalin.

At the other end of the tunnel another steel door opened a crack. We could see only part of a face wrapped in a towel.

"Don't take any pictures until we tell you," a voice from behind the towel said.

"I won't," answered Frank. He held up both hands and the camera hung from his neck.

The door opened. We stepped inside and were hit like a two-fisted punch by the smell. It made us gag. It was overwhelming and sick. The stink of excrement and urine had replaced the air. I forced myself to breathe through my mouth.

The lighting was dim and smoky and the men moving around us were part of a scene of what hell probably looks like. When the Pope said there is no such place, that hell is only in our hearts and minds, he was not entirely right.

"If you're cops, you're dead," said someone very close to my ear.

Except for that, it was quiet. The crowd of inmates was staring at us. Some had towels protecting their heads, some had blankets wrapped around their heads and bodies. Some had broom handles with sharpened ends pointing toward our faces. Some had knives made of sheet metal. All of them were staring at us.

One gave an order to open the way and the others stepped back. Two inmates with spears slid behind me, and others also armed with pointed sticks moved behind the other reporters. I felt a sharp jab in the back of my neck.

"Move," they said.

As we walked, groups of inmates parted to let us pass. We walked along narrow corridors in front of cells, all with men both inside and out of their cages, some gripping the bars, but all staring at us.

They were exhausted. Most had torn clothing. The smell became more intense. Excrement was smeared on the walls. Then I saw one face as we passed. Our eyes caught. He was in his cell a few feet from me. He was white, in his early twenties. His face was beaten and his lips were bloodied and swollen. I turned to keep eye contact with him, but a spear jabbed into my neck and pushed me on.

We were led over a catwalk in single file. I still felt the tip of one spear, but now just brushing the back of my neck. Below us were three tiers of cells, each with men looking up at us. Everyone in there was paying for crimes. Some, the better-looking ones, the smaller and weaker ones, were paying dearly. Few could live a normal life when they got out.

At the end of the catwalk a group of inmates parted to reveal five men sitting on the floor in front of a cell.

"You can talk to them," we were told. "Take their picture, but point the camera right at them and don't raise it."

Frank took half a dozen shots, then was told to stop.

"Now talk," an inmate with a spear told me.

With all the questions I wanted desperately to ask I could only get out, "How are you?"

One of them, a guard with red eyes, three days growth of beard and dry lips said, "Fine. We're fine. Tell my wife I'm okay."

I asked his name. "Mike Pace," he said.

"Mine's Frank Berniac," said the guard next to him. "Tell my wife I'm okay, too." He added that the hostages were kept apart and were kept moving around the prison.

I got each of the other hostages' names and the same comments, then an inmate stopped me and the other reporters from asking more questions.

"That's enough," he said. "You see they're okay."

I looked at the men whose eyes were pleading that I should know other things. But we were backed away and a group of prisoners closed in around the hostages. We were led out a different way than how we came in. The walk went faster. No one spoke. The spears were held close to our necks. At the exit a steel door was opened for us and one inmate said, "You tell them we haven't hurt the hostages, yet."

We stepped into a tunnel and the door clanged behind us. In front of us another one opened. We walked out a rear exit into the cold pre-dawn air. Behind me Frank said, "I almost wet my pants." I thought I had too.

We told the police about the hostages and described conditions inside. They would not have to wait to read it in the papers. When you can help someone stay alive you don't hold back information. Except I didn't tell anyone about the money in my pocket. When you are very, very dumb you keep that to yourself. Then I left for the newspaper office.

By eight a.m. I had written the most dramatic story of my life and Frank's pictures were ready. They showed five men huddled together with tired, frightened faces. At their sides were the legs and hands of some inmates.

When the city editor arrived I told him about the night's adventure. He was pleased. Then I took a subway downtown to school.

As I did most mornings, I arrived in class needing a shave and smelling of too many cups of coffee. Most of the other kids thought I worked on the fish docks. My first class was sociology. I was ready to contribute my views of prison life. Another student requested we talk about the riots, but the professor, a woman with a freshly awarded doctorate, refused. "It is just too terrible," I remember her saying. Then she added something about newspapers sensationalizing the events and the need to stick with the study of established principles of human behaviour. Such was school.

But I wasn't really sure what she said because I was just too tired and I thought if I told them where I had been it would be grandstanding, so I let it pass. School was for theory and that is very important; the streets are reality. I would get a degree in school because it was an official mark of accomplishment. But I would get my education from the street.

Early in the afternoon I got home to my wife Valerie and our two kids. Going to school full time and working full time is not possible without an understanding mate. One probable reason why our kids were able to read so young was she read to them through the afternoon and again after dinner so I could sleep.

At eleven p.m. Valerie woke me and fed me, and we said good morning and good night and I walked into the dark to take the subway back to work. On the newsstand I picked up a paper. The front page was filled with the picture of the hostages and the headline over my story said: Our Reporter Takes a Long Walk in a Dark Place. Below it was my byline. It was almost embarrassing. On the subway I looked at those reading it. I watched their eyes to see if it held their attention. It did. I felt good.

That night I was back at the same prison, but this time something was happening. Police ranks had swelled and other men in heavy jackets and work clothes were arriving by the carload. Some had shields made of tabletops and chair bottoms. Some carried football helmets. They were prison guards and they told me they were going to free their friends.

Car trunks opened and the axe handles inside were passed out to the guards, who now numbered several hundred. Then an unmarked police car pulled up and the trunk of that was opened. It was filled with new police nightsticks, wrapped in cellophane sheaths. The sticks were nearly three feet long and made of hickory filled with lead. They could crack open a skull with little effort.

The nightsticks were passed out to the guards and in a few minutes the street was littered with the long, thin cellophane bags rolling in the breeze.

The reporters asked questions, but there were no answers. The guards moved like an army around to the back of the prison. The police kept the reporters from following. We were told we would be briefed soon.

I left the group of reporters and walked a block away from the prison, then turned a corner and made my way to a row of factory warehouses overlooking a wall around the rear of the prison courtyard. It was five a.m., and under a streetlight I met one other person, a long-haired reporter working for the *Village Voice*. The paper eventually evolved into a respectable chronicle with thoughtful articles on social issues and excellent music and theatre reviews. But back then its editorial position was a reflection of that reporter: tie-dyed shirt, beads and peace buttons. He had the same idea as I did: very simply, to see whatever it was they didn't want us to see.

We talked a night watchman into letting us into the building and climbed stairs through dim, mostly empty floors until I wound up on the fourth floor. I lost track of the other reporter.

I looked out a window and could see down into the prison exercise yard. The battle inside was over. We later learned the fighting had been short and vicious. The guards stormed in through a back door swinging their clubs. The prisoners fought back with their spears and knives, but the guards kept coming, protected with their makeshift wooden shields and with a strength of purpose that the prisoners could not resist. Once the guards had broken through the prisoners defending the entrance they charged along the cell-blocks swinging at everyone in their way. The prisoners began dropping their weapons and ran back behind their bars for protection.

What I was looking at from that factory window was what happened after the guards had got control and the hostages had been rescued. What I was seeing was the punishment handed out. Two rows of guards, about thirty in all, stood in parallel lines in the exercise yard. No one on the street on the other side of the wall could see them. They held clubs. The rear door of the prison opened and an inmate was pushed out. He was hit on the back with a club. He went down, then was picked up and hit again. He fell, but was pulled to his feet and was forced to walk between the rows of guards. When he fell again he was beaten. When he got to his feet, trying to protect his head with his arms, he was beaten on his ribs. The clubs hit him over and over until he collapsed at the other end. Even from where I was I could see he was drenched in blood. He was dragged away and thrown on the ground alongside the prison wall.

The next prisoner was brought out and pushed into the gauntlet. Then the next, and the next. I stared in disbelief. I tried to take notes, but after a brief description of the scene there was nothing else to write. The words were the same: "A prisoner is hit, hit again, again, again. He gets up. He is beaten to the ground. Up again. Beaten again." I stopped writing. I could only watch as the bloodied, limp prisoners were thrown into a pile. Some of them tried to resist going through the gauntlet. They were beaten more severely.

I felt very much alone. I still didn't know where the other reporter was. There were no telephones near the windows and I could not leave what I was watching to look for one. And I felt the helplessness of realizing that calling the police would do no good.

When the beatings stopped, I left.

A crowd of reporters gathered around the front steps of the prison. They were listening to John Lindsay, the mayor of New York, giving a press conference. He was telling them and the city that the riot was over, the hostages were released unharmed and that "there was no retaliation. I give you my word," he said. "It is all being handled orderly and peacefully."

From the back of the crowd I blurted out, "That's not true. The guards were beating them."

This was a major mistake. Reporters do not tell other reporters what they know. In a business where information is the only product, the only way to improve the product is to have more of it and have it more accurately than the competition. My competition now held microphones at my face. I could not change my words. I could not escape, and I was young and angry. So, in short, I gave away my story.

One of the millions to whom it was broadcast while he was driving to work was Jack Smee, the metropolitan editor of the *Daily News* and my boss. He did a double take at the radio. "Damn him," was all he said.

When I arrived in the city room I was met by a phalanx of senior editors who did not look pleased. They knew the publicity was great since I was called a *Daily News* reporter on the radio and people would be waiting to read the story. But I was a junior reporter and this might involve major lawsuits. They wanted to know exactly what I had seen, how many guards, how many times were the prisoners hit, how long was I there, how far away, did I have counts, did I have numbers, did I take notes? Without using the word, they wanted to know if I was exaggerating.

The previous story from inside the prison had brought me some recognition. They wanted to know if it had gone to my head. The *Village Voice* reporter I mentioned being there left some room for credibility. He was not, after all, a *New York Times* reporter.

I was angry with them for questioning me. They were hard-nosed, trying to prevent truth from being shaded by a young reporter's emotions. But I saw them as The Establishment siding with the police and guards. It was a confrontation in which I knew I was right, but I knew I had no supporting evidence.

Then the bell on the wire photo machine began to ring. It did not stop ringing and from across the room the photo editor called to the men who were interrogating me.

Pictures of what I had described were coming out of the machine. I did not know that one floor below me in the factory, an Associated Press photographer had been at work. The first pictures showed two lines of guards with clubs and a prisoner falling between them. More pictures spilled from the machine into a holding tray. They showed a pile of bodies next to the wall of the prison yard. The next picture showed guards with clubs hitting a prisoner. More photos came showing guards with clubs dragging inmates across the ground.

The editors looked and shook their heads. Then in a scene straight out of Hollywood, one of them said to me, "Write your story, kid."

I wrote it, said goodnight at nine-thirty a.m. and took the subway downtown to school. My first class was French. Some mornings academic life was anticlimactic.

The result of it all was I read about myself in the *New York Times*, prison guards looked up my home phone number and threatened me, the prestigious *New Yorker* magazine mentioned me, and a New York grand jury indicted seven guards for brutality. All were eventually acquitted when neither the photographer nor myself was able to identify any individual faces.

Dinner for One

There are now so many courses on how to relax, you could get stressed out just trying to decide which one to take.

There is the deep-breathing way and the meditation way and the exercise way and the massage way. And then there was the Sid Klein way. He taught me how to relax even in the middle of the most chaotic situation imaginable.

Sid was a rewrite man on the *Daily News* and I met him when I was a copy boy just starting out in the newspaper business. Sid was one of the old-timers who wore a green sun visor over his eyes and his sleeves were held up by rubber bands. His job was to listen by telephone to reporters on the scene of a breaking news story and then to write the story as fast as he could. Deadlines were always just minutes away.

The paper, at the time he and I worked there, dealt mainly with crime and disaster and scandal. The page one story was almost always a murder, and the most foul and ugly murder possible. That was followed by a fire with people trapped on the top floor. And if there was any political news it was about an elected official who was caught either in a brothel or taking a bribe.

In short, the world Sid thrived in and the one I was learning about was an endless tale of corruption and crime, all of it put together in a noisy office of telephones and manual typewriters where people shouted, "How many dead?" and "You've got two minutes to deadline!" and "If you're wrong about those facts, you're fired!"

It was a world where stomachs could get very knotted. Except for Sid's. He worked nights, I worked nights. For most of us who worked nights, dinner was a sandwich that we half ate before going back to work again. Between changing typewriter ribbons or whatever we'd wipe our fingers, grab a few more bites, then go back to work again.

Not Sid. When his dinnertime came he pushed aside his typewriter. He took a white linen tablecloth out of his desk drawer and spread it over the top of his ink-stained and cigarette-scarred desk. He then pulled a plate, a wine glass, silverware and a linen napkin out of that same drawer. He carried a regular construction worker's lunch pail, but out of it came pieces of chicken, French bread, potatoes, and a small dish of salad.

From another drawer came a bottle of wine. This was back in the days when people could smoke and drink in their offices, especially newspaper offices. There was lots of drinking in this office, but no one else had wine. Sid would pour himself a glass and eat in total peace.

All around him typewriters were still beating out late-breaking sex scandals. Reporters were still yelling for copy boys. Editors were still yelling for writers to write faster. But Sid might as well have been in an oak-lined booth of an exclusive uptown restaurant. Around him adrenalin was pumping but he was in his own world, quietly salting his chicken.

When he was done with his meal he took a bottle of brandy from another drawer and poured a small glass. And then he lit a cigar. After dinner he cleaned his dishes in the men's room and folded up his tablecloth and put it back in the drawer. Then he slid back his typewriter, put his headset back on and said into the mouthpiece to the frantic reporter on the other end of the line, "How many bullets? How many dead?"

I don't know if he ate like that because he simply liked eating like that, or if it was a part of a plan to relax. He never told anyone. I just know that I remember his meals better than my own, and also that he was one of the few people in that business who didn't die of a heart attack.

The Terrible Fate
of the Best Story Ever Written

Most often the only way you know something is good is when someone you never would believe would say it, says, "That's good." That's how I knew my story was good: Chilly, who worked on the copy desk, told me it was good.

Chilly was a copy editor. He was brilliant. His right hand was shrivelled with arthritis and he always had a pipe in his mouth and he was always in a hurry. But he could take a badly written story and, by changing only a handful of words, he would make it sing. That was his job. He didn't write, he fixed writing.

Compliments from Chilly were rare, and hard to understand because not only did he have that pipe in his mouth, he also mumbled. So you had to be quick to catch him. But he looked at me, pointed to the story with a pencil in his left hand and mumbled "Good."

I have written seven thousand stories for television and have forty pounds of newspaper and magazine writing. But the moment when Chilly said "Good" gave me a feeling of pride that I never had before, or since.

The story began on a hot night in 1972 when some Vietnam vets took the Statue of Liberty as a hostage to protest the war. If you are going to do something you should do it in the biggest way you can, and there is no bigger hostage in America. My city editor told me to go and see what this was all about.

I headed downtown on a night when hundreds of thousands of others across the country were protesting the war. But no one else held Lady Liberty as a prisoner.

The vets were wearing the same camouflage fatigues that got covered in mud in the rice paddies of Vietnam, but instead of guns they brought a heavy chain and a big padlock and when the statue was closing for the night they forced the security guards out and locked themselves in. Then, from the top of the torch, they hung the American flag upside down.

They weren't going to hurt the statue. They weren't going to blow it up. They just wanted to make a statement that they had been to Vietnam and they didn't think it was a good idea that any more should go.

In the streets of America, citizens were going to war with each other over the issue of the war. Hundreds of thousands were protesting it, while hundreds of thousands were threatening and cursing the protesters. The college I was going to in lower Manhattan was invaded by wrench- and pipe-swinging construction workers after students held an anti-war protest out on the sidewalk in front of the school. The workers smashed in the front windows and glass doors of the school. Families across the country were shouting at each other over the dinner table. Going to Canada to escape the draft could get you called both a hero and coward within your own family.

Most of the reporters, editors, photographers and writers at the *Daily News* were against the war. One hundred and fifty of us tried to buy a full-page ad in the paper we worked for as an open letter to Richard Nixon telling him to stop the war.

However, the publisher's policy of the paper was to support the government. It was good business to back those in power, so in the eyes of those who owned the newspaper the government was right and the war was just. The publisher refused to run our ad.

So the employees of the *New York Daily News* took their business to the *New York Times* and bought a full-page ad. It announced that the undersigned *New York Daily News* employees—reporters and editors and photographers and writers, many of whose names the public knew well—urged the president to stop the war.

In the White House, Richard Nixon was pounding his desk over the cowards who disagreed with him. Veterans taking over the Statue of Liberty he took as a personal kick in the groin. "Get those bums out of there!" he supposedly said, but that was erased from the tape.

I loved assignments like this. It was not a case of the office organizing a helicopter to get me to the statue. And it was not a case of calling officials of the government or police or supporters of the protesters for comments. It was, simply, go and find out.

How I found out would be my own business. But there was a problem. It was two a.m. and the regular boat that goes to the statue had stopped running. The island on which the statue stands is owned and administered by the federal government, and it wasn't allowing any unauthorized boats to dock. The statue was lit up, two miles away across the water. There were tourists taking pictures with instamatic cameras that would later churn out prints that were all black except for a small pinpoint of light, but at least the tourists would be able to say they were there.

I walked up and down the edge of the waterfront until I saw some tugboats. They work for shipping lines that pay them huge amounts to pull freighters in. But this was New York.

"Hey, you guys going to the statue?"

"What you want to know for?" a deckhand replied with suspicion.

"I'm from the *Daily News*. Would you take me?"

Tugboat people loved the *Daily News*. They liked the gritty reporting and the racing forms.

"Jump," they said.

I didn't ask why. I didn't care. I leaped off the dock, landed on the deck and they pulled away a minute later. But despite my swelled head, I just had good timing. I was in the right place at the right time and asked the right question. All dumb luck. They were taking another man to the statue—a federal park ranger who had been flown in to tackle the problem.

He wore a Stetson hat and a uniform that was crisp with a razor-sharp crease in the pants. He stood alone on the back of the boat and I stood near him.

It was breezy that night and cool on the water. The lights of lower Manhattan sparkled like the Milky Way. You cannot see the stars from lower Manhattan because there are so many electric lights in so many windows that they blot out the sky. But the sight of that man-made galaxy coming from cloud touching office buildings is magnificent. The ranger, Robert Dunnagan, one of the few law enforcement officers of the National Park Service, stared out across the inky black water at the lights and said, "My God, how do they live here?"

He told me he grew up on the open ranges of Wyoming and worked in Yosemite National Park in California. He had never seen anything like this. He had never seen more than a few people per square mile. Then he said he didn't know much about the politics of the fellows who had locked themselves in the statue. "They are just youngsters," he said. "I don't think they will cause any problems. We'll just listen to them."

I spent the night with a dozen other reporters on that lonely island with New York glittering over the water, and when the sun came up I hitched a ride back to Manhattan.

Back in the office they had some big-time reporters with Washington connections working on the story. The boss asked me what I had and I told him there was a little story about the man who might solve the problem.

I wrote it in three hundred words, which is about one page in this book. I wrote that the "US park ranger was on the back of a tugboat on the inky waters of New York harbour. He stared at the lights of lower Manhattan and said, 'My God, how do they live here?'" I wrote about his Stetson hat and his uniform refusing to flutter in the breeze, and I wrote about him saying, "They are just youngsters . . . We'll just listen to them." It was so simple: Write the facts and fill them with humanity.

I handed it in to the city editor and walked back a few steps, then I turned and watched him read. If there had been an earthquake in New York at that moment I would not have moved.

The city editor smiled. Then he put my byline at the top. He wrote *my name* on it. Good God, the ranger may have been impressed by a lot of electric lights, but I was getting *my* name on a story in the largest circulating newspaper in America.

Then the city editor called "Boy!" He shouted that loud and with authority. When copy boys hear that, they jump. They jump or they get fired, union or no union. I had spent four years listening to that shout and jumping and hoping someday I would be the writer of some of those stories I was carrying. Now I was. I was still young and bylines were infrequent. But here was a glorious one.

The copy boy brought the two and a half pages, triple-spaced, to the copy desk, where Chilly grabbed them with his left hand. He puffed. He skimmed his pencil across line after line. He put in some commas and took out some words. Then he looked up at me. He knew I was there. He pointed to the story with the pencil in his left hand and mumbled "Good."

A half hour later, at nine in the morning, I went to school, and then home to sleep with dreams of having written the world's most wonderful story. At midnight I was back in the city room, staring at my byline at the bottom of page three, which is the most-read page in a tabloid.

Now I have to give you some background about newspapers in 1972. They were still the main source of news for most people. There were seven papers in New York. The nightly television news was fifteen minutes long and consisted mainly of someone looking down at papers and reading stories that were mostly taken from newspapers. The *Daily News* had five editions a night plus two minor revisions, meaning they could change page one or page three or five so that they would keep up with whatever was happening throughout the night. It was exciting to read the paper. Things were happening.

This rapid-fire news production was accomplished by having reporters who worked on the street, or in city hall or police stations or fire halls, who just reported. They were aces at getting to scenes of crime or devastation or corruption quickly and getting the scoop and then getting to a phone. Most of them could not write. Few if any of them could type. But they were experts at collecting the information and flavour of an event. They had names like Stich and

Monk and Greaser. And they knew where every phone in the city was.

While the event was happening they would be reporting it, right from the scene of the political rally or bust of the illegal booze joint. At the other end of the phone was the rewrite man. They were all rewrite men, even the women. They had headsets over their ears and manual typewriters under their hands. They were tough—no artistic writers here. And they knew the words that were tough. They could listen to a story and turn it into a two-fisted, bare-knuckled or eye-wetting tale of a dead soldier, crook, cop or cat before the reporter was finished talking.

It was an amazing process. Often the event, the fire or the politicians arguing or the prize fight, was still going on while it was being written up. The copy boy stood next to the typewriter to pull out the page after three sentences had been written. He gave it to the city editor who checked the facts and substance of the story, then it went to the copy desk to tighten the writing, and then on an old-fashioned conveyor belt it went down to the composing room. There, banks of linotype operators with gas-fed fires blazing in their giant type-making machines began setting the first lines of the story into metal type. The fire melted ingots of zinc and this scalding-hot liquid would be set and hardened into lines of print, one line at a time. From there the story went to the printers, who set the lines into a metal page form, or galley, again one line at a time. Often the first few lines of the story had been converted into lines of cooling metal type being squeezed together by the ink-blackened fingers of printers while the reporter on the scene was feeding more events to the rewrite man.

In 1972, newspapers still left television in their dust.

This is the way newspapers had been written since the '20s, when competition made it necessary and telephones made it possible. It was in this world that I began work, but I was at the very last whisperings of it. I was in the first generation who were told that television would change newspapers and we would have to change. We who were young would have to learn to report the story, and write it. Two jobs for the same pay? Is that legal?

I didn't care. I was looking at page three with the headline Dark Voyage to the Lady with the Light, and my name under it. They could ask me to do anything tonight—change a typewriter ribbon, get coffee, anything—and you would hear no complaints.

"Go over to rewrite, young fellow, and listen to Stich," said the city editor to me.

Stich McCarthy was from Ireland. He liked to drink. He took many advances on his paycheque so he could keep on drinking. His face was red and lined with tiny veins, which he didn't care about because to get rid of them he'd have to stop drinking and drinking was the only passion he had, besides reporting. He knew many cops in the city and got fantastic stories of horrible crimes. He only came into the newsroom to get money; his real office was at the back of police stations and inside bars and at the scenes of horrible crimes. And the latter turned out to be where he was now calling me from.

He told me of the slayings of three men and how this connected with an underworld war, and he told me the names of the men and how they died and how many guns they were carrying and which mob the police were hunting down for questioning. All of this while the bodies were still on the street.

Luckily Stich McCarthy is now dead. If he had to wait for a police press conference in the morning he would take up drinking full-time, which would not be good for his health.

I wrote the story pretty much as Stich told it to me. He didn't waste time with fluttering breezes or descriptions of how bullet holes can ruin fancy suits. A copy boy took the first page I wrote to the city editor, who wrote "by Philip McCarthy" at the top of the story. How Philip became Stich was like how Charles became Chilly. If you asked you would be told, "because that's what people call them."

Stich got the byline because it was his story. I expected that. I was still learning and it was an education just to listen to him. He had spent a lifetime looking at crime and he specialized in murders, which still intrigued him. He missed no details. He knew how to get information and how to give it. He was a good reporter. Plus I felt good because the city editor looked up at me and said, "good job." That was two compliments in one paper. This would be a day I would not forget.

But over at the news desk where they laid out the paper, they had a problem: where to put this new story for the second edition. Something had to go and they were looking at page three. All the stories on it were about the Statue of Liberty. The main one was about the event itself. A second story was on the White House reaction to it.

And there was that third story, the sidebar about the park ranger. I saw it in slow motion. I saw the editor take his heavy black pencil and put an X through my story. I saw them pick up a blank dummy page and write, in the spot where my story was, the words, "new story, mob murder." No one looked up at me; there was no sympathy or regret. It was big-city news and the mob murder was more important and more current and more exciting than a park ranger on the back of a tugboat.

But on the other hand, of all the stories I have done, only the occasional one took on a personality of its own, almost becoming a friend. This was a story that came to life, and then perished. It came, it went. It is not Shakespearean, and it will never be looked at in schools, but when I am dying I will remember, "My God, how do they live here?" and say to myself, "Chilly liked it."

The Art of Climbing and More of What They Don't Teach in Journalism School—But Should

A valuable lesson in journalism is learning to climb steel poles. It once helped me get a story and saved my life.

Reporting is more than asking questions and being able to type. It is getting into a situation so that you can ask the question, and then getting *out* of the situation so that you can type up your report. The situation I was in was halfway up the steel pillar of an elevated train track with the back of my pants split open. A train was going by overhead, my feet were slipping and on the street below me a gun battle was going on.

This was Brooklyn, 1973. Four men had held up a sporting goods store and police got to the scene before the men were able to escape. This would normally be a good thing, a fast police response so that the bad guys could be put in jail. But in this case the bad guys had rack upon rack of high-powered rifles and uncountable boxes of ammunition. They also had hostages. Sadly, the first two policemen who jumped out of their car in front of the store had been shot before they took two steps. One was killed; the other lay on the ground, wounded.

Pedestrians on the street screamed and scattered as a second police car screeched to a stop, then a third and a fourth. Women with baby carriages crouched behind cars. Old men and women who had been shopping in nearby stores were hiding behind rows of soup cans. Screeching tires and bullets make a terrifying noise.

A few of the second wave of police crawled out to their fallen friends and dragged them behind a car. They ripped open the shirt of the wounded man and tried to stop his bleeding. Another cop tried frantically to breathe life into his dead comrade. More shots came from the store and pounded into the sides of the police cars. The police fired back and the front windows of the store shattered.

The shooting went on for several minutes. Roughly fifty bullets flew back and forth across the street while more sirens howled and more police arrived. They drove over the sidewalk to get around the knotted street traffic. Before the fight started, the street had been crowded. It was still crowded now, but no one was moving.

A bellowing voice came from the sporting goods store: "We have hostages!"

The police stopped shooting, and except for sirens in the distance the street grew silent. Slowly the cops moved their cars into position to make a barrier. Ambulance crews had taken away the dead and wounded men. And now there was nothing but a dozen blue and white cars with the heads of policemen peering over the hoods, their guns aimed at the store.

"Are you coming out?" one of them yelled.

"Are you joking, man?" one of the robbers yelled back. "We have twelve customers in here. They'll die before you get us."

More sirens. And now the surrounding streets were being choked with police cars. Some officers tried to lead pedestrians to safety. Other police worked their way into stores that were in the line of fire and told the customers to stay back and make themselves comfortable. They would be there a while.

The police Emergency Services Division arrived with bulletproof vests, high-powered telescope-sighted rifles and grappling hooks. They were the forerunners of the SWAT teams. The Emergency Service cops were the specialists who rescued people trapped under subway trains, or shot with deadly accuracy at men holding bombs and threatening to blow up classrooms of children.

Last on the scene was a high, windowless van that snaked quietly through the streets and parked half a block away. It was the command post with radios, maps, telephones, an electric kettle and a large jar of instant coffee. Less than an hour after the first alarm had come in, the battle lines were set. A cornered gunman is dangerous. Hostages give him unmerciful power.

A cop stepped out of the van and made his way up to

the barricade of squad cars. He was the negotiator. He put a bullhorn to his mouth, but he only got out the words "I am lieutenant—" before the sides of the cars were hammered with bullets. Tires exploded and flattened.

He put down his megaphone. "It will be a long day," he said and walked back to the van.

Throughout the city, editors had heard the first reports on their police radios. Photographers who scan the airwaves and cruise the streets were already there. This was a story of fear and desperation. This was not sensationalizing. This was reality turned to hell that could happen to anyone. It would get very big play because it was an unfolding drama of life and death and it would not wait for any police briefing later on.

I was one of the first people there because I just happened to be close. I was working in Brooklyn police headquarters at the time. Behind me came dozens, then scores of reporters who were sent to see what was happening and tell the story. I had been out of the Air Force only a few years. In uniform I had suffered only a few broken toes when some machinery fell on my foot. Now, back in my hometown, I was entering a war zone.

I got there amid growing confusion as the crowd swelled and traffic was rerouted. A block away there was a circus atmosphere. People came out of the low-income housing projects and lined the barricades. They had not been shot at. They felt no fear. It was just another event, like an accident or a fire, that would be entertaining and give them bragging rights for being there. Some of the teenagers carried radios and danced on one side of the wooden barriers while police stood on the other side. I passed this crowd; my press pass got me through police lines. I walked down a side street then through a back alley and came out on Broadway, the street with the sporting goods store.

It was dark, even at midday. Overhead was the elevated train, the "El," which is actually an endless railroad bridge supported by steel girders. The El in New York is almost three storeys high, and the steel supports are planted deep in the sidewalks on both sides of the street. Along the sides of the El are tenements that become walls and turn any street with an overhead train into an endless dark tunnel. The only light that makes it to the street comes through the slotted wooden ties on the tracks.

Then I heard a shot.

"Oh, my God," I thought. I could not see where it came from. I was alone in the middle of the street and I saw the guns of the police over the tops of their cars. I started to run back but there was another shot. This time I could see it came from the store. I took another step and heard someone scream, "Get down, you fool."

I did not go gently. I did a full body slam on the cobblestones and my fingers tried to grip the edges of the rocks. I heard the crack of more shots to my right, where the store was, and heard the thud of impact into the cars to my left. I was lying on top of an old streetcar track and I tried to push my nose into the slot so I could get even lower.

The shooting stopped and I moved, crawling backwards, with just the power of my toes and my fingertips. I had crawled under live fire once before, in basic training. But this was different. They weren't trying to miss now. I came up beside a cop lying behind the wheel of a car and wearing a black knitted fisherman's hat. He held a rifle with a telescope aimed at the store. It was pointing over the spot where I had been stretched out.

"From now on you might like to stay behind us," he said. He did not take his eye away from the telescope.

I telephoned what information I had gathered to the city desk at the *Daily News*, and then added the tale of my adventure.

"That's just fine," said the editor sarcastically. "Get yourself killed and you'll upstage the story." The editor was from Belfast, where he had been a reporter and had seen and written about hate and violence. "You see things and you report them, that's all you have to do. And try to stay alive until you do it," he said.

Good advice. He was the same editor who once saw me come back from a story with a wad of notes, which I was shuffling through trying to write a story. "You should be able to cover the second coming of Jesus Christ on the back of a book of matches," he said. Ever since then I observe more and write less.

On the second day of the siege I was sent to replace the overnight crew. The ranks of reporters had grown. The hostages were still inside and negotiations over the telephone had been going on all night. The same police hostage negotiator who had been there at the start of the ordeal was sitting on the back bumper of the van. He was drinking black coffee from a plastic cup. He had been up all night, sparring with his wits, jabbing with tones of voice into a telephone while his unseen opponent taunted him to come and get him, "but be ready to slip on the blood when you do."

"It's trust," he said. "You've got to convince someone who knows you are conning them that you understand them. You can't be phony and you can't promise things you can't deliver." A good negotiator is both a chess player and a street fighter.

I don't know why he talked to me. Maybe it was my dimples and I looked friendly. Maybe he needed a break from the tension and I happened to be nearby. But I loved that moment. I remember thinking what a terrifying situation it was. One person was dead, a dozen others might be dead, more people for sure were going to get hurt. But right now I was talking to someone who knew all the decisions were his, and he wasn't afraid. It was an honour to be sharing the same air with him.

While doing other stories I have met many people I liked. There was the woman raking leaves in front of her house on West 10th Avenue in Vancouver. She was so happy. She was fighting city hall to save the trees on her block.

We talked for fifteen minutes before I learned she had had cancer, and had beaten it, and now she was trying to save trees. And there was the biker with a big gut and scruffy beard who volunteered to walk dogs at the Vancouver pound. He always picked the dogs that no one else wanted to walk, the ugly ones, the ones who looked like no one would ever claim them. He took them out for some freedom and exercise, and while he walked he sang lullabies to them.

Meeting people like that is a huge reward for just doing my job.

Meanwhile, back at the siege in Brooklyn, the reporters waited through long hours with little seeming to happen. Each worried that we would have nothing to add to our stories when suddenly shooting erupted from the store. The police returned the fire and shot tear gas through the shattered glass in the front. Ambulances wailed nearby, screams came from the streets behind us, and then the bullets came our way. Rounds were hitting the sidewalk and sides of the buildings. We were nearly a block away, but the gunmen were firing wildly out of the storefront and down both sides of the street. The onlookers and reporters dove for cover, behind cars, in doorways and behind that forest of steel girders that hold up the El. One more policeman was shot and we later learned that one of the robbers was hit in the stomach.

I looked around and saw the best route of safety for myself was something I had done as a boy. I grabbed hold of the vertical steel girder and climbed, my hands pulling on the sides and the edges of my shoes pushing on the rounded heads of the rivets that line each girder. I stretched up to go two rivets at a time and I heard the back of my pants split. Right over the sound of bullets: *Rrrrip.* Damn, I thought. I wasn't making much money and I only had two pairs of pants for work.

But at least I was up here and they were down there. I

was twenty feet over the street. Every kid in New York who grows up in the boroughs where they still have elevated trains learns to climb those girders. You look like you are on a South Pacific island going up a coconut tree, except you are on a ramrod-straight beam and over your head are trains ten cars long carrying thousands of commuters.

When you are a kid it is a scary, dangerous, thrilling adventure. When you have two kids of your own waiting at home and you have gained weight and your arms aren't used to the exertion, there is no thrill. My hands were sweating and the steel I was holding onto vibrated as a train passed overhead. In other cities the trains would have been stopped. Not in New York. To stop the trains would be like plugging up an elephant with diarrhea. The city would explode.

Then the police started moving in, car by car and the bandits poked their rifles out the front door and began firing wildly. Something had gone wrong for them. I later learned that the hostages had escaped through a secret passage that led to the roof and when they were gone the robbers knew they had nothing to bargain with. Besides, the penalty for killing a cop in New York is death. Two of the robbers thought it would be better to face the cops while they still had guns rather than in court when they were in shackles.

Bullets were flying out the front of the store. The cops behind me were firing back. It was then that I prayed, "Please God, do not let them lift their eyes to You, or me."

In five minutes that seemed like five hours it was over. Tear gas rolled in and the robbers came out. They were all in their twenties. I came down from the girder. I tried to hold the back of my pants together with one hand but I was young, and image was very important, and I thought it would look like I had messed my pants because I was afraid. So I tried to get information and take a few notes while standing with my back against a wall.

Back in the office, while doing the story with my pants stapled together, I described the episode as I had seen it from up the pole. "It sounds like you had a good view," the editor from Belfast said.

"I did," I said. "And I followed your rule. I didn't get killed."

If I ever teach in a journalism school I will have a mandatory course in pole climbing and crawling backwards, with extra credit for fence hopping and banister sliding. Academics are necessary, but it is the practical skills that will give your stories a little better insight and help keep them from being praised posthumously.

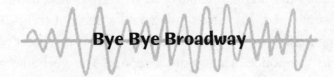

Bye Bye Broadway

New York then was not as peaceful as it has since become. In the early 1970s, three hundred people a year were killed by stray bullets. In poor neighbourhoods mothers put their children to bed in the bathtub. It was the only bulletproof place.

My wife Valerie had a window view of the crime. In the first apartment we had after I got out of the Air Force, she watched muggings on the street below. The first was horrifying: an old man walking alone was hit from behind by a youth who knocked him to the ground, kicked him and ripped his wallet from his pocket, tearing away half his trouser leg. It happened so quickly no one had time to react. Others were on the street, but no one went to his aid until he was down and the attacker had escaped.

"Maybe this isn't such a good neighbourhood," Valerie said.

She saw other muggings from the window. Police said there were one hundred thousand violent street crimes in the city each year, although everyone knew that figure was not accurate since many were never reported to police. My mother was mugged. My father-in-law had a gun put to his head during a robbery. But why report it? What is the point? You talk to the police. They write a report. You go home with your bruises and torn clothing, minus your wallet, and that is the last you see of the police until your neighbour is mugged.

One evening a few weeks later, when Valerie was alone with our two small children, there was a desperate pounding on our apartment door. She looked through the peephole and saw a frail old man being attacked by three teenagers. The other doors in the hallway stayed closed. Valerie opened ours and went to his defence with elbows and nails. She is a tough woman. The young attackers ran off. Muggers, even in groups, are not used to anyone coming to someone else's aid. Mugging is a safe business with the odds entirely on the attackers' side. Tilt the scale even slightly and they will go after weaker prey.

Another time Valerie was with our kids in a park, which was actually a concrete playground with benches, swings and a basketball court, and it turned out drug dealers were on one side of the playground and the police were on the other. With no warning they began shooting at each other. She grabbed the children and covered them with her body. The firing was over quickly. It was a small skirmish that would be continued somewhere else. Valerie was frightened for herself, but enraged for her children. "They should not grow up here," she said.

Shortly after that I was with both kids in a laundromat around the corner from our apartment house. Across the street was a grocery store. As if on cue, while we were washing our clothes, gunmen held up the grocer. Police arrived and there was shooting. I pushed the kids behind a washing machine. The shooting ended; we picked up our clothes and went home. "We are moving," said Valerie.

And we did, to a safer neighbourhood. But then came the final straw. She took our kids to a children's birthday party. Four- and five-year-olds played games and the father of the birthday child brought out the cake with five candles burning on it. He was a policeman, and although he was off duty on this day, when he put down the cake his jacket opened and Valerie saw the handle of a pistol sticking out of his waistband.

Her eyes widened. "Do you always carry that?"

"Always," he answered.

Soon after that I read a story in *National Geographic* magazine about British Columbia. It had pictures of the sea and mountains and smiling people.

"Read this," I said to Valerie.

She did.

"Let's move," I added.

"Okay," she said.

We were going to Canada, to trade gun smoke for fresh air.

Canada? When You Hit the Pacific, Just Hang a Right

Several months later we had all the ingredients for a life change. I had a job at the *Vancouver Sun*, which I got the old-fashioned way with a resumé sent by mail. We had the government paperwork, and I had rented a U-Haul truck for three days. That was all the time I figured we would need. Like most Americans I had slender knowledge of Canadian geography. We had driven many times to Montreal and we loved being there, and we knew we would be happy in Canada. The drive to Montreal from New York took eight hours. I knew Vancouver was west of Montreal. So I figured one day to drive the truck to Montreal, one day to drive west to Vancouver and find an apartment, and one day to return the truck.

On the morning we left New York City, Valerie and I were sitting in the cab of the truck with our kids, Colleen and

Sean, squeezed in between us. The motor was running. We had all our possessions in the back, including Valerie's childhood piano and last year's Easter eggs.

An aunt and uncle of Valerie's came to see us off. Her uncle handed me a map. "You may need this," he said.

I started to unfold it like an accordion. It stretched wider and wider. My eyes opened wider and wider. It spread across both kids and now Valerie was holding the other end. In front of us was a red, mapped-out line that stretched from ocean to ocean. My jaw fell.

I wish I were exaggerating. I wish I were just trying to make a joke, but it was, sadly, true. I had no idea where Vancouver was other than west of Montreal. Except for basic training in the Air Force, I had never been west of New Jersey.

"Good luck," said Valerie's uncle.

We left and I just missed hitting a parked car.

"Can you really drive this?" asked Valerie.

"Cross your fingers," I said.

"Can we listen to the radio?" asked Colleen.

Like most people who grew up in New York, I knew as much about cars as I did about Canada. People in New York don't need cars. There is no room to drive a car and no place to park it when you are not driving. I grew up staring into the dark tunnels of the subways, always riding in the first car so I could watch the tracks and the bare light bulbs flying by underground. Forget all the horror stories you may have heard about the subways, the screeching wheels and the characters and the crowds and the speed make for an exhilarating ride. And you don't have to park it.

But before our wedding day I thought I should have a licence so I could impress my new bride by driving her home from the church. So I went to a driving school and signed up for a three-hour refresher course. I was twenty-two and had never sat behind the wheel of a car in my life.

In the first hour they taught me how to make it go forward. In the second hour they taught me how to park. In the third hour we reviewed the first two hours. From there I rented the driving-school car for one more hour and went straight to the motor vehicle testing station and took my driving examination. I made the car go forward, I parked it. I passed the test.

"My uncle will drive us from the church," said Valerie.

Now here it was, seven years later, and I still had never driven anything larger than a Chevy with a rusted-out bottom that I had bought for $150 in the Air Force. But this time I was sitting behind the wheel of a large moving truck.

Over the next ten days we plodded west, hardly getting up enough speed to feel any wind on our faces because this was 1973 during an oil crisis. We drove across the US because that's what route the map showed. But the Arab nations were feuding with the western nations over money and the result was that gas stations ran dry no matter what map you used. There were traffic jams at every pump. In America, no station was allowed to sell more than ten gallons of fuel to any vehicle. The tanks on our truck took forty gallons. The truck got ten miles to the gallon.

"Sorry. We have to stop again."

But the kids didn't mind. Like slingshots they were out of the cab every hundred miles, sticking their arms inside Coke machines and looking down into grease pits and squirting water on each other from hoses that were supposed to fill radiators. Oil embargos make travelling a lot easier for kids.

After the first two days we discovered our budget did not stretch as far as the map. No more money for motels or restaurants. So we pulled off to the side of the road and ate canned peaches and canned pears for dinner, then slept under the truck.

A week later we stopped in Vancouver, Washington. "Look, the map is wrong," I said to Valerie.

"My uncle gave us the map," she said. "Follow it."

Half a day later we were looking at the maple leaf flying over the words Canada Customs: Stop and Report.

"Do you have any guns?"

The twenty-something Customs inspector standing near the Peace Arch stared at me. He did not say welcome to Canada. He did not say good luck, do you have a job, glad to have you, do you like the Canucks?

"Well, do you have any guns?"

"No, that's why we are coming here. To get away from guns."

"We just had a priest come up," said the inspector. "He had a gun."

"We don't have any."

The inspector searched the back of the truck. He looked behind the piano. He looked under the Easter eggs.

He saw himself as part of the first line of troops protecting his native land from invaders. We saw him as the bad witch in a fairy tale. He was following his training manual. We watched him as he rooted through our belongings, apparently determined to find something.

"What are these for?" he said accusingly.

He was pointing to the cable spools that had once held wires. We'd found them abandoned on the streets in New York.

"They are our tables," we said. "We like rugged furniture."

"Are you sure that's what you use them for?"

"What do you think we use them for?" I asked.

"I'm asking the questions."

It was at that moment Valerie and I thought of making a U-turn and leaving. But then suddenly the inquiry was over. The young inspector made some notes in a book, handed us our paperwork and said only, "You may proceed."

I am sure that young inspector is now an old bureaucrat in charge of hunting down laughter and happiness, and is doing an excellent job of it.

So we rolled into Canada. It looked beautiful. It was clean and refreshing and all the people we met seemed to be making up for the inspector. Everyone was friendly. But there was a slight problem. In Vancouver in 1973 there was little new construction going on and most people lived in houses, not apartments. We were looking for something to rent and there was a zero vacancy rate. As a result we wound up living in a tent at a campground in White Rock, miles south of Vancouver, for more than a month. Every day Valerie took the kids and went hunting for a place with walls and roof that we could live in and I went to work at the *Vancouver Sun*.

Mixed Media: Rewriting a Newspaper Guy

The trouble with getting on the road to a big, bold, happy, optimistic change in life is that sometimes you hit potholes, and you get shaken up and you wonder if you got lost. If you want to stick it out you have to learn to drive on this new road because the road isn't going to change. You have to adapt.

The *Vancouver Sun* was the beginning of a series of culture shocks. In New York I was used to being told by editors, "There's a bombing in Greenwich Village. Get going, and be out of hearing range before I finish this sentence." Or I would wander into detective squad rooms in police stations where the newly arrested were kept in cages in the middle of the room and cops banged out reports with two fingers on manual typewriters. It was there that I got stories, first from the cops and then from the accused, who shouted back at the cops that it was all a frame-up. It was a lively existence.

On my first morning with the *Sun* I found in my mail slot a stack of assignments to check. Each of them had a note saying it had been checked by the night shift and nothing new could be found. Under that note was another note, saying they had all been checked by the previous day shift and nothing new had been found. My first thought was "Fire the day shift and the night shift."

Then the reporters went to lunch. Everyone got up at the same time from the newsroom and went to the company cafeteria and it seemed everyone took the same seat each day.

"Heavens to journalism. I think I have a problem," I thought. I was just a young, incompetent-at-spelling reporter, but I had never seen a group of reporters stop reporting to *eat*. Never. Sure, one or two might stop to chew, but not all of them. There had been no cafeteria at the *Daily News*. Editors who worked inside ate at their desks. Reporters who basically were not allowed into the building—"How can you work if you are not where the story is?"—ate standing up on a sidewalk, usually a coffee and a pretzel for breakfast, lunch or dinner, depending on what time of day it was.

I was invited to join the group. They were kind, they were polite, they included me in the conversation. I asked, "What if something happens and we are all eating?"

"Probably nothing will," they said, "and if it does, the afternoon shift will get it."

And they were right. Most of the news in the early 1970s had to do with politics and labour. There were strikes and threats of strikes. There were elections and threats of elections. The news was largely plans of group actions and then actions of the groups. And most of that news was gotten over the telephone.

"Whoops," I thought. "I am in the wrong place."

A few months later there was an opening at the police station. I took it and went down to the old building near Main and Hastings. It was much more comfortable there, and for the three years I worked at the *Sun* I never went back to the main office of the newspaper.

But there was more adapting to be done. On my first night shift while I was heading for the building at 312 Main Street I heard from behind, "Hey, you. Stop."

I turned around. It was a cop. "You know you could get a ticket for that."

I turned around again to see if he was talking to someone else.

"For what?"

"Jaywalking. You know that's against the law."

"What! Are you *serious*?"

"Are you giving me a hard time?"

"Are you joking?" I replied.

Here was a true clash of cultures: not language, not religion, but ways of life. I was used to dodging cars and getting across a street whenever there was a three-second gap between bumpers. Where I came from, cars didn't always stop for lights and pedestrians seldom waited for walk signals. The friendly policeman, who was just doing what he had been taught, knew the rules were there to be obeyed and things worked better when they were.

In my heart I could not believe I was being stopped for

illegally crossing a street. That's not a crime. A crime is shooting and fighting and hurting. The cop in his heart could not believe that someone was being defiant when he had been caught in the act of blatantly breaking the law.

We talked. We worked it out. I didn't get a ticket. He walked away worrying about the calibre of new immigrants to his country. I walked away wondering if I would fit into this new world.

The crime rate in Vancouver then was low. There was one policeman who supposedly carried chocolate bars in his holster. But anyone who suffers any kind of painful, unprovoked, unexpected injustice is hurt just as much in Vancouver as in New York. A window broken on a car is not a big crime, but it sure hurts, and the victim feels helpless and infuriated and the fact that it happens should be recorded as part of the passing history of a people as much as the good things that are done. The story of a youngster whose parents did not care when he was caught shoplifting is just as important, maybe more so, than the story of a murderer. Knowing how the seed is planted and cultivated can teach us more than wondering later why the tree was rotten inside.

I wrote about crime in Vancouver, big and small, for the *Sun* for three years, then one day Alyn Edwards, who was a reporter for BCTV and also worked out of the police station, asked me if I had thought of working in television.

Well, no, actually I hadn't. TV to me was trite. TV was what you laughed at when you thought of news. Newspapers were the only *real* way of getting a story. TV relied on pictures and sound clips. Newspapers relied on reporting.

But for the experience, I went to the TV station's newsroom. This was the old newsroom, before they built the large, modern one we now work in. Back then it was a spare room in the basement, which you entered through a screen door that had come from a corner grocery store and had a sign that said Drink 7-Up. Inside the reporters wore blue jeans and some had long hair and they sat on piles of newspapers instead of chairs. The only desk was a long plank of wood that was nailed into a wall and held up by two-by-fours. The editors worked in airless closets with bare bulbs over their heads and black curtains behind them. This was no-frills journalism.

They seemed like a family. They seemed rough. And most of all, they seemed dedicated to beating the CBC, which then had a larger audience.

Okay, I thought, I like this.

"Not so fast," said Keith Bradbury, who was the assignment editor. "We don't know if we really want you. Can you find stories?"

A challenge, I thought. I'll show this guy.

"Here's the deal," I said. "I come up with five original stories, all making page one in the newspaper over the next five days, and you give me the job."

"Yeah, sure," he said, apparently thinking it was not going to cost him anything to watch this long shot fall on his face.

Early the next day I was waiting outside the homicide and robbery squad room before the detectives showed up.

I was waiting for Sam Roberts, the sergeant in charge of

all the violent crimes in the city. He was large—fat actual-ly—with sleepy eyes. But on one side of his brain he could think like a criminal. On the other side he thought like a cop. Once the crime was in his thoughts there was no escape until it was solved. His detectives went to crime scenes, observed and asked questions. They poked and uncovered evidence. They dug and scraped through the ugliness of a place that was usually in a shambles and often soaked in blood. Then they went back to the police station and told Sam what they'd learned. He asked questions and they answered. He sat back in his wooden chair and closed his eyes and asked about obscure corners of the investigation. He asked what relationships victims had and he asked if windows were opened or closed and if clothing was folded or thrown in a pile.

Then he made suggestions on what could be looked at next. He was the conductor of the crime-solving orchestra. He put pieces together and, like a real Sherlock Holmes, he simply deduced. In the end, when most of the guilty were caught, it all looked so obvious. Of course, now I see, that is why the criminal did it and how he did it and how he thought he would get away with it, until Sam thought about it.

I loved listening to Sam work. He was the starring char-acter in an incredible novel, except he was living and breath-ing and squeaking back and forth in his old wooden chair.

"Tell me something," I said. "I gotta know something, *anything*, but it's gotta be good."

"First, tell me what you see in this room," he said. I was there with four other detectives. Two of them had their jackets off and were wearing shoulder holsters. "You tell me what you see that's different and I'll give you a tip."

Is this the way news is found? Is it a game? Is it a contest? Is that fair? Of course it is. Things have value according to how hard you work for them. If gold were easy to come by, it would be plastic.

I looked around the room. This was the old police station with file cabinets and wooden desks and rotary dial phones. I scanned the walls and the faces of the detectives and the chairs two of them were sitting on and their suits and trousers—and I stopped.

"What do you have to tell me?" I said.

Sam knew I had won. I was looking at a detective who, like all of us, got up before the sun was up and, since he didn't want to disturb his wife, he dressed in the dark. And when he did he had put on one brown shoe and one black shoe. But he did not know it and he *still* did not know it until he realized that Sam and I were both looking at his feet.

He looked down and was as embarrassed as any guy who sees dead people and violence and cruelty for a living can get. His face wasn't quite red but it wore a strong "oh, stupid me" expression.

Sam had seen him when he walked in, and had said nothing. He did not know he could use that information later as a contest for me. And he had not embarrassed the poor guy when he spotted it. He just held the information. That is the mark of someone who has a talent, a strength, and knows how to control it.

"You know about the terrible murder of that ten-year-old girl?"

"Yes, of course," I said.

"We believe she was killed just on a bet, a dare, by some other kids."

"Oh, God," I said.

The world is like that. Fun and games are followed by death and disgust.

They were within a few hours of verifying it completely, too late for the final deadline of the *Sun*, which was then an afternoon paper. He gave me a head start, time for me to get the background of the case and talk to other detectives and write the story, and hold it in case it was not true. He trusted me.

This was before there was a police spokesperson who delivers the news after it has been screened and capsulized. There was an informal meeting of reporters with the deputy chiefs each morning, but basically you had to find the stories through contacts and through reading endless police reports, ninety-nine percent of which were minor crimes.

I called the *Sun* and said I had a big, sad, shocking angle about the death of the little girl, but I could not tell them more until it was verified. I told them it would make them shake their heads, if I could get it in time.

They gambled and held a space for me. Five minutes past the deadline I was in the homicide squad room waiting for Sam, who was waiting for the phone to ring. When it did, it shattered the silence and made me jump. Sam listened for a minute then hung up and said to me, "Go ahead with your story. She was stabbed to death on a bet between two teenagers."

The story was already written. I phoned it in to the office. It was a shocking story, so sad and disturbing that to think of it now, when that child would be in middle age and have children of her own as old as she was when she was killed, is still heartbreaking. Those who read it that afternoon would have a sick feeling in their stomachs. Does that make a good story? No. It makes a tragedy. Is that important? Yes, if you want to understand our human condition.

By the time it was delivered to the newsroom of the TV station it was too late for them to get the story. It was only an hour before the newscast. All they could do was call the police and confirm the story was true and report that the *Vancouver Sun* said it was true.

Are these kinds of stories necessary? Do they actually have to be told? By God, yes. If I were the victim I would want it shouted. I would not want a death like that to go unmentioned, hidden as though it did not happen. It disturbs the universe. It is not right. It does not make for a happy day, but I know that not to acknowledge the evil in the world as well as the good is a crime of fear and ignorance. There is no way to fight the evil if we say it is not there.

There is another thing hard to justify. That story helped me get a job in television. It was the first of five consecutive stories that went on page one of the newspaper. The others were not as dramatic: they concerned vice and gambling and the seizure of guns. But they were all gotten the same way, by determinedly stalking the hallways and squad rooms of the police station. Each one wound up being read in the news-room of the TV station as a fresh tale that they did not have. By the end of the week I was offered the job of TV reporter. Eventually I got to the point where I could write about but-terflies and flowers and little kids playing in puddles. But that came later. On my first assignment I went right back to reporting crime.

One Second

The first day on the new job at BCTV I was down in the bomb shelter where Abby Drover was held prisoner. She was the twelve-year-old who was captured by a sick nutcase on her way to school. For six months she was held prisoner under the garage of a house in Port Moody. Her tormentor starved and abused her, and then he pretended to help police and other neighbours search for her. It was hard to suspect him.

You may or may not believe in a God, but the way Abby was freed was on the edge of being beyond belief. The man who abducted her, Donald Hay, had been fighting with his wife. This was six months after Abby had disappeared and was presumed dead. Hay threatened several times to kill himself and each time he locked himself in his garage. He had covered all the windows with black paint. Only he knew about the bomb shelter that had been put in twenty years earlier by a homeowner who was afraid of a nuclear attack.

To get to the shelter that became a prison you had to go into Hay's garage. Then you had to open cabinet doors under a workbench and crawl through the doors. Behind them was a trap door in the floor. From there a shaft went ten feet straight down. It led to a door that was heavily padded. Inside the door was a concrete cell six by eight feet and in there was a bed frame with handcuffs attached to it. Abby had been held there for exactly one hundred and eighty-one days.

On the day Hay was fighting with his wife, he was as usual depressed. He told her he was going to kill himself. He went out of the house and locked himself in the garage. His wife took him seriously this time and called police. When they got there they looked through a spot where the paint had peeled away from a window in the garage but saw nothing. They could see everywhere inside and there was no one there. They told Mrs. Hay that the door was locked and the garage was empty. Her husband must have gone somewhere else.

She begged them to check again. At the same moment, Hay was coming up out of the bomb shelter. He had crawled out through the cabinet doors and was standing inside the garage when, through a crack in the window, he saw the two cops walking his way. He dove back under the workbench and got all but his foot through the cabinet doors. One of the policemen just saw the shoe disappearing. It was there for only one second and then gone.

The two cops broke in, but by that time Hay had gotten down the shaft and was back inside the bomb shelter with Abby and apparently sure he had escaped detection.

The cops squeezed under the workbench, pulled open the trap door and went down the shaft. They knew they would find Hay there. They did not know what else they would find.

"Oh my God," said the first cop when he pulled open the door to the bomb shelter.

The window of opportunity of finding Abby had been one blink long. If the cops had looked one second later, Hay's foot would have been inside the cabinet door and they would have returned to the distraught woman with the assurance that the garage was empty. If they had grabbed Hay before he got to the workbench they would have taken him away for psychiatric observation, and he may never have mentioned that he was holding a little girl prisoner underground. Her remains might still be down there.

One second. One blink. Something made the cop look at that spot under the workbench in that instant. We are not going to try to figure out what or how. But the fact is he looked.

That was my first day on the job. Someone else did the story; I was just along to see how television was done. But because of this job I was able to go down into that dank prison cell. There are things you can learn about the incredible strength of the human spirit just by getting the chance to look at an overflowing chemical toilet, a bed frame, some handcuffs and a jar of water. The human spirit is very strong.

Of Hookers and Hamburgers

O ver the next few years I covered crime and the courts
in Vancouver. One case in particular concerned the
lengthy battle between the police and Joe Philliponi. Joe ran
the wildest nightclub in the city, the Penthouse. The police
said he was living off the avails of prostitution. He said he
was just operating a nightclub and could not put labels on his
customers.

Joe had started out as a coal miner in northern British
Columbia, supporting his mother and younger brothers and
sisters. When he moved to Vancouver he lived in an apartment above a storefront on Seymour Street and invited the
city's night citizens to join him at home for a drink after the
rest of the town had gone to sleep. He called his apartment
the Penthouse, sort of as a joke. It was only two storeys up.
But that was the birth of the nightclub.

By the time I got to know him he was sixty, short and

tough with the grip of a young weightlifter. He also had the reputation of being the godfather of Vancouver, yet the only crime he was eventually convicted of was charging prostitutes a two-dollar admission fee each time they came back into his club. Inside, a woman would pick up a customer, then leave, finish her business at some hotel, then come back to the club and pay another admission fee. Joe never got anything off the prostitutes except the price they paid to come in, the same as all the customers paid. But those two-dollar fees were judged to be enough to convict him of living off the avails of prostitution and he was sentenced to one day in jail.

The other result of the conviction was that prostitutes now had nowhere to go, except the street. Before Joe went to jail there had been no hookers in Vancouver's neighbourhoods. Prostitution was controlled in a way no legal minds could ever have devised. After the conviction, and continuing to this day, neighbourhood groups are left to fight something that did not exist when the Penthouse and other nightclubs were considered houses of sin. Back then the prostitutes stayed dry and warm and out of sight of schoolkids.

While I covered his case I got to know Joe and one day he said he had a clean act, meaning no strippers on stage, just country music for a change, and would I like to bring my wife and kids?

"Well, sure." That's great, I thought. Take my kids to the Penthouse, which was the equivalent of a tour to the forbidden land, a place people only whispered about. It would be an experience. "Sure. We'll be there."

That night, Valerie and Colleen and Sean—the kids

were then in grades five and six—and I stood in line outside the Penthouse. The crowd looked rough and sleazy, sort of a cross between extras in an old gangster movie and gamblers in Las Vegas at three a.m. Many eyes looked down at our kids. Kids just didn't go to the Penthouse.

On the walls outside his office Joe had mirrors angled so he could look up and down the block without sticking his head outside. He spotted us and this squat, lumbering man came down the stairs and walked along the line of customers. They stepped back to give him room. You don't block the way of a godfather.

He introduced himself to my wife and kids, then took Colleen and Sean by the hands and led them past the crowd and inside. The club was already packed. He snapped his fingers in the air and pointed to a spot next to the stage and, in a moment, someone brought a table and suddenly there was room for it.

Then Joe Philliponi, the man who police said was the closest thing to the king of the underworld that this city has ever had, put a towel over his arm and took orders from my kids. They both asked for hamburgers and milkshakes. I don't know how his staff supplied those drinks—perhaps someone did some fast running outside to an ice cream parlour—but shortly afterwards, Joe came back with a tray of burgers and shakes and served them to my kids.

He was no crook. He was a hard-working man in a tough business. He never married or had kids. He said he never had time to. He had to support other relatives in the only way he knew outside of digging for coal.

A few years later he was shot through the head during a robbery. I still miss him. And it is only because of my job that I got to know him as more than a reputation.

It was also during this period that I got tired of death. In one year I saw sixteen freshly killed people. There was the man in a Skid Road hotel stabbed to death with a pencil through his ribs. There was the woman who came home from bingo and was raped and murdered in her garage. She lay on the cold concrete floor with her skirt pulled up, dead. Her husband of many years went into an unbearable silent depression and will probably never allow himself to heal.

There were many others. The bodies of the teenagers taken out of a car that had overturned in a ditch. They were stiff and contorted when they were pulled from the water. They lay near my feet. My heart was breaking for their parents, and for all parents of children who die.

And there was the old fellow who went missing from the retirement home near Marine Drive in south Vancouver. There was a search for him and I did a story about that. When he was found, I was working nearby. He was dead, lying near some blackberry bushes. While the cameraman and I talked to the cop who was at the scene I started picking and eating blackberries. It was hot and they were sweet and gave me energy. It was macabre. How can I be eating blackberries next to a dead man? Well, of course there is nothing wrong with that, except there must be something wrong with it.

The first murdered person I ever saw had been beaten to death behind the newspaper office in New York. He had been killed only a few minutes before I was standing next to his bloody remains. It made my stomach sick. Now I was eating berries near a dead man. It was time to change what I did for a living.

Any police reporter, just like any cameraman or police officer or fireman or medic or soldier, has the same stories, which is why so many of them joke about death. Sometimes that is the only way to deal with it. But other reporters are lucky. For their own sanity, or at least for mine, I altered what I wanted to report about. Slowly, I started doing more stories about stray cats and kids hunting for tadpoles. There will never be an end to crime and hate and tragedy and disaster. There is no end to those shot through the head during robberies or killed in car wrecks. But others who are younger and tougher are lining up to do that work. I have found my heaven in the daily search for people planting seeds or pruning trees in their backyards. It is good to join them for a few minutes and share stories of carrots and guinea pigs and baseball. And you don't have to be a reporter to do what I'm doing. All you have to do is walk down the street and stop when you see someone painting a fence, and say hello. A sane life has a balance to it, and I am spending the second half of mine trying to fill up the good side of the scale.

What's Behind Those Stories?
I: A Tale of Two City Slickers

"**W**hat's that?" Ken Chu asked. He was pointing to a couple of furry creatures. Ken is a TV cameraman who grew up in Shanghai and Hong Kong and the only wildlife he had ever seen was Godzilla in the movies.

"Raccoons," I said. However, my basic knowledge of wild animals comes from New York, where the wildlife is pretty well limited to pigeons and rats.

We were standing on the top of a hill and Ken was pointing to the bottom, from which the furry creatures were now looking up.

"Raccoons aren't that big," he said.

We were two guys who had had childhoods on concrete and we didn't have a clue about what goes on in the woods.

"We should get a picture of them," I said.

We had been hiking along the crest of a hill in a remote

wilderness in central BC, one hundred miles from the coast, after filming a story about a family that lived in isolation so deep that radio signals did not reach them. They had a life I had dreamed of when I was growing up. They were frontiersmen, self-sufficient farmers and hunters. They paid no taxes, saw no utility bills and stood in no lines. In my imagination they were so close to heaven they could almost jump up and grab hold of it.

The woman, whose name was Trudy, had written a book about the wholesomeness of life in the wilderness and the news director had read it and said, "Now here is a family that knows how to live. That would make a good, warm-hearted story." He handed me the book and told Ken and me to put them on television. A day later we were chartering a small float plane that we found at the end of a pier in Bella Coola.

"Do you go to Lonesome Lake?" I asked. That was the family's address: Lonesome Lake, BC. Now, that's some address.

"We'll try," said the pilot, "to get you anywhere you want."

He flew the plane using his legs to steer and his hands to hold a map that showed only mountains and lakes. There were no radio towers for guidance, no houses or roads for landmarks. It took an hour to spot the homestead hidden in the forest. We circled several times to let the occupants know visitors were coming, then we landed on a lake.

It was about a five-mile walk from the lake, but it didn't matter. This was the kind of story I wanted to do. I was putting crime and inhumanity behind me. Now I could get involved with the lives of honest, hard-working people.

We saw the house. The family was coming out. Ken started filming them to get the excitement of first meeting.

"Turn that camera off! Who the hell do you think you are?" shouted the man who was in the lead.

"We're from BCTV," I said smiling, trying to win their approval and break this small impasse. "We would like to do a story about you."

"And what's in it for us? And who invited you?" said the man. He wore soiled clothing and a long beard and looked more like a peasant of the mud than a prince of the wilderness.

"Publicity for your book," I said, trying to sound positive. I still didn't know his name, but I assumed since Trudy had written about her husband Jack that this must be Jack, and the woman behind him who wore big rubber boots, a big dirty coat and a crewcut, must be Trudy.

Trudy stepped forward. "Why didn't you tell us you were coming?"

"Your book says you only get mail four times a year."

"So, what's the rush?"

Then Jack, who still had not introduced himself, spoke up. "Let's get this straight. You get paid for being here. Your television station makes money from showing us. Even the pilot makes something. What do we get?"

Six million square miles of wilderness surrounded us and I felt like I was in a Brooklyn pawnshop arguing over the value of an old bowling ball.

"Well, besides the publicity," I said, "you get the chance to make others feel good about the lives you lead. It says in your book you are warm-hearted, loving and that this is a beautiful place to live." I was almost pleading. "It's the kind of story that would relieve the drudgery of many others' lives."

"No deal," he said, and he and his wife turned around and began to walk away.

In a flash of horror I imagined the news director's reaction. "You spent *what* getting there and you came up with *nothing*? They are nice people, I read their damn book. What did you *do* to them? And also: you're fired."

"Wait," I called after them. "Is there anything we can do?"

They stopped, turning in unison. "Pay us."

"I can't do that. We never pay for stories. It's not done."

They shrugged and began walking away again.

"Wait." They were getting farther away. "Let's talk about it."

Again they turned, looking like players in a poker game.

"We have to do the story," I pleaded. "We spent a lot just to get here."

"Then you shouldn't mind spending a little more."

"But—"

"You can write it off as expenses," Jack said. "Just slip it in as a cost of doing business."

I gave in. He had a royal flush in his hand, I had nothing. "How much will you charge us for a tour of your farm?"

"Twenty dollars—each," he said. He gestured to their

daughter standing back at the house. "That'll be sixty dollars."

I borrowed some of the money from Ken, then paid the man.

"Now you can take pictures," he said.

They walked with us around their farm, they weeded a garden, and Ken filmed them. We asked if we could see inside their home, but Trudy said, "That's not what you paid for."

She also said she was annoyed that the publishers of her book had changed some things. She wanted it to be a factual account of the care and feeding of swans on their lake. "They added that romantic stuff about living in the wilderness."

We left, and I left some idealism behind. Jack asked us for the newspaper that was stuck in with the camera gear and as we walked away they were huddled tightly around it. This was not going to be an easy story to tell.

It was a two-hour walk back to the lake where the plane was floating and we were on the crest of that hill when we saw those furry animals. They were by a stream and so apparently could not hear us at first.

Then we looked ahead and saw the pilot desperately waving to us. One hand told us to stop. The other hand had a finger across his lips. He pulled it away and silently mouthed the word grizzlies.

We looked down the hill again and I realized the small animals were much farther away than I thought, and not so small. Our guide pointed to some nearby trees, the size we could climb. I looked down again. The bears looked up. There were three of them. I had only seen two at first. I missed the larger one, the one that was the mother of the other two.

They started running up the hill, directly toward us, and in an act that separates news people from the rest of the sane world I pointed to Ken's camera: "Can you shoot them?"

"*You* shoot them," he said and shoved the camera at me.

"No, you," I said, and pushed the camera back.

The bears were halfway up the hill. They were coming fast. Because their front legs are shorter than their back ones, bears run up hills faster than on flat surfaces. Ken put the camera down. "We are going to die."

"The trees!" we heard the pilot shout. He was a safe distance away and already climbing one.

The nearest trees were only a few yards away. They had grown among boulders the size of cars. I banged my shins climbing on one, sliding on the moss, then grabbed for a branch. I was wearing boots that I got in the Air Force. They were made for walking on tarmac and runways, not for gripping slippery rocks. I do not know where the strength came from, but even with my feet slipping on the bark I managed to pull myself up—and just as I did, one of the claws of the mother bear came down on the rock that my foot had just left. The huge black claws stretched out from the dark fur and scratched the stone. Then the claw went back to the ground, and after only a slight hesitation, the bear ran off with her cubs.

Ken and I stared at each other. We were about twenty

feet apart and fifteen feet off the ground. His eyes were wide. He was shaking. I was shaking.

"I think we can get down now," I said.

"No."

"What do you mean, 'No'?"

"I'm not getting down."

"They're gone."

"How do you know?"

Good question. I squeezed the tree and didn't move.

The pilot came back and looked up at us. "You can stay if you like, but I'm leaving."

We half ran the five miles back to the lake and Ken kept threatening the life of the editor who had sent us. When we got to the water's edge, Ken and I walked right out into the lake to the bobbing aircraft.

"We could pull it in," said the pilot, who was on shore holding a rope attached to the plane.

Bella Coola had only one street then, one Chinese restaurant and one rough hotel, and by the time we had changed into dry clothes everyone on that street and in that restaurant and hotel knew about us. When we walked into the restaurant, the tough, savvy local folks started laughing and applauding.

We had gotten our story; it just turned out to have two sides—the one you saw on your television about a family in the wilderness, and the one those folks in Bella Coola are probably still slapping their knees over, the visit of the fools from the city.

What's Behind Those Stories?
II: Jailbird Journalists

One summer in the mid-1970s, Eric Cable and I travelled along the Alaska Highway looking for stories. Eric is a large man who looks like he belongs in the backwoods, or in a bar in the backwoods, which is often where he was to be found.

We stopped in Fort St. John, near the Rocky Mountains in the northeast corner of BC. After checking in at a motel Eric suggested we visit the local beer parlour, which he said would be a good source of information. There was no music, no atmosphere other than smoke and worn tables with lumberjacks sitting around them. Two older men sat at a corner table. One looked like a bulldog, squat and powerful. His companion was thinner, with a stained cowboy hat and a deeply wrinkled face.

"Can we sit with you?"

"If you have reason to," said the bulldog.

"We'd like to buy you a beer."

"That's not your reason."

They do not waste words. We told them what we were looking for.

"I know some who you might find interesting," said the man with the hat. "I fly supplies to them."

"Where do you fly?" I asked.

The imaginary fingers in my head are crossed. Say something good, please.

"Anywhere you pay me to."

That's good, I like his attitude. Attitude is good in a story. Now, please again, there is a silent prayer to the story god. Please let him have a story to go with the attitude.

"Been doing it long?" I asked.

"Thirty years."

It is almost music now.

"All up here?"

The questions are shorter now. If finding a story is like sex, this is the heavy foreplay.

"Yep."

Oh, my gosh. A true northern bush pilot. The story hormones are surging.

"Anything unusual happen?"

"Crashed," he said, "five times." He looked at me and tilted back his hat, and I could see three fingers on his right hand were crippled. "And lived," he added.

Bingo. Contact. Story coitus.

His name was Jimmy Anderson, sixty years old and now

giving birth to a living tale about a real person. Good stories are not planned in an editor's office. They do not come from press releases. They emerge suddenly and unexpectedly and grow spontaneously on their own. They are born when someone says, "Oh, my gosh. Really? I didn't know that. Wow. I don't believe that." A good story has its own life, and dictates its own terms.

Jimmy Anderson was an independent bush pilot. He worked for no company and the more daring he was—meaning the more risks he took with his own life—the more money he made. He was one of the last of a very select group of men and women who had a plane for hire and flew to places and then worried about how he would land.

"Would you take us up?"

There is always the practical side to a story for television that newspapers don't have to deal with. A good newspaper reporter could sit in that bar for an hour and, with a little verification afterwards, have a story of adventure and romance that would make every reader want to be a bush pilot. A ride would be better, but a good reporter could make the beer parlour his cockpit.

In television you need the aircraft, and it has to fly.

"Might," he said. "If my plane's ready." It was being repaired at a field outside of town.

He took a drink of his beer, then said, "Let's see."

Four of us squeezed into his pickup truck and drove through the night to the airstrip. He stopped and his headlights lit up the plane. The nose was missing. Wires stuck out of the cowling. The engine was lying on a workbench.

Jimmy walked slowly around his aircraft, touching it, studying it in the beams of the headlights. The only things he owned on this earth were his Cessna 180 and his Ford pick-up.

"It's not ready yet," he said. He looked back at it with sadness.

Eric and I were disappointed, but we felt more sorry for Jimmy than ourselves.

"But if you still want to go for a ride," Jimmy said, "I'll get a plane."

"How?"

"Borrow one."

In the cities of the south you borrow a magazine or five dollars or a book. In the north, you borrow an airplane.

He drove us back to town. It was after ten p.m. and he said he would pick us up in the morning. Eric and I went for dinner, then Eric told me it was his birthday.

I groaned. Eric is a rugby player. On an ordinary night out of town he would find reason to celebrate. On his birthday he would tempt new limits.

He headed for a beer parlour. I followed. This time he was not going in search of stories. We drank. We toasted his birthday. Then we went to another beer parlour and did the same. It is surprising in a small town how many places there are to escape isolation.

Then we went to a disco—a disco in 1976 in Fort St. John, which was a barn with a stage at one end and a bar at the other. The place was crowded, with cowboy boots stomping on the floor and a loud country band playing rock.

The guitarist still had grease under his fingernails from his day job. The tables were crowded with big-shouldered loggers swallowing beer in gulps and on the dance floor were girls in cowboy hats, tight jeans and sneakers. These girls drove trucks and chainsaws in the day and at night they could handle any man in this place.

Eric and I watched sneakers dancing with steel-toed work boots and we toasted his birthday some more. At two in the morning they got out the brooms and told us it was time to go home. We staggered out into the foggy night with only a slim idea of where we were. We could see a green glow in the distant sky and assumed that was the neon sign over the Holiday Inn where we were staying.

Arm in arm we stumbled across a field in front of some warehouses, getting our feet stuck in the mud and singing, when a police car pulled up in front of us. Another skidded to a stop on our side and a third pulled up to box us in. Royal Canadian Mounted Police got out of each of the cars.

"Don't move," said one Mountie.

We lurched and held onto each other.

"What are you doing here?" asked another.

"Going to our hotel," I tried to say clearly but I wasn't sure if I understood my own words.

"Put your hands against the car," said the first Mountie.

"What did we do?"

"Shut up."

"I want to know what you think we did." I tried to sound indignant.

I was answered by being thrown against the car and

searched. Eric was also searched, but when you are as big as he is they don't start by throwing you against the car. Then we were told to get in the back of one of the police cars.

"Not until you tell us what you're arresting us for."

"We're not arresting you. We want to talk to you."

"Why?"

"We think you know why. Now get in."

He pushed me into the car on one side and Eric got in the other.

"We're from BCTV," I said as the door slammed shut. I might as well have said we were from XYZ. I did not know that the signal from the television station covered almost the entire province, except back then, for technical and geographic reasons, it did not reach one town: Fort St. John.

The back seat of a police car is a mobile prison. There are no handles on the doors, no way to roll down the windows, there is not enough room for your feet and there is heavy steel grating in front of your face.

The Mountie got in the front seat next to the heavy-gauge shotgun in a rack beside his leg and said without looking around, "Don't do anything stupid."

You jerk, I thought as he started the car. "Are you going to tell us now why you're arresting us?" I said.

"You think about it," he replied.

Eric folded his arms and sat sideways so he could stretch out his long legs in that small space.

"Happy birthday," I muttered.

The Mountie flipped on his overhead red light and stepped on the gas. The wheels spun in the mud. He tried backing up and then going forward, but the wheels kept spinning. I felt the car going down.

"Damn," said the Mountie and he punched the steering wheel.

"It's probably the extra weight in the rear," said Eric.

"Don't get smart." The Mountie was angry.

The other two policemen got out of their cars and tried pushing while the red light turned on top of the car, lighting up their faces. The driver put the car in low gear and pushed slowly on the gas, but the wheels spun again and one of the Mounties in the back cursed as mud sprayed his uniform.

"Want me to help?" asked Eric.

"Just shut up," said the driver.

I sank lower in the seat.

After several more attempts to free the car the cop behind the wheel turned around. "You still want to help?"

Eric smiled. He would smile at his own executioner. He got out and I got out. Eric put his big hands under the bumper and with the help of the other two policemen pushed the car out of the hole.

Thanks a lot, I thought.

The men thanked Eric, then opened our prison door and we climbed back into our cage. Some cameramen only take pictures. I was with one who helped us go to jail.

On the way to the police station our guardian got a radio message that confirmed that there were two persons from our TV station in town and their description matched ours. In New York I had a press card with my picture issued by the police department. It is a criminal offence to counterfeit it. In

Canada, things are less formal. You say you are a journalist and you are taken at your word, usually.

All three cars pulled over to the side of the road and the cops got out and conferred. They told us there would be no need to question us any further and suggested that we go for coffee with them at an all-night diner.

While I bought coffee and donuts for half the Fort St. John detachment, we learned that there had been several break-ins at the warehouses. We had walked by them and looked as though we were pretending to be intoxicated.

"No one else in town would be stupid enough to be out in that field in the middle of the night."

Just before four in the morning we were driven back to our hotel. I lay down with a throbbing head and sick stomach and, totally exhausted, fell asleep. Three hours later there was a pounding on my door.

"I've got a plane. Are you coming?"

I would rather die. I crawled off the bed and opened the door.

Jimmy Anderson, with his cowboy hat, stood in my doorway. "Well, let's go. You wanted a ride. I'll give you one."

He took us to a farm outside of town and there, in a field with cows, was an airplane. It was homemade, he said. It was painted white with a red stripe around the middle and it had been painted with a brush. There was bright red tape on the wing. It was big enough to carry two, one in front and one behind.

"Get in," he said to me. I thought my stomach was going to come up.

I stepped over cow patties, climbed on the struts and tried to squeeze into the rear. It was tight; my hips pressed against both sides of the plane and my knees were jammed into the back of the front seat.

"You should be able to fit. I carried a mule in this once," Jimmy said. "Tied up his legs and squeezed him in."

We took off by bouncing off the field and my stomach got sicker. But as bad as I felt I admired his flying. It was as though he was the machine and the machine liked being part of him. His body leaned to the side and the airplane followed. My stomach fell and I was sicker.

I tried to ask a question, but he interrupted me. "I used to take hunters out and spot game for them."

"That's not fair," I shouted to him over the engine noise. Then I realized this was not a good place to be critical.

"You're right," he shouted back. "I was warned by a game warden. But I was younger. What I used to do," he added, "was find caribou in a clearing like that."

He banked sharply and we looked down at an empty field.

"Then I'd shut off the engine so I wouldn't scare them, like this."

He turned the key and the motor stopped. The propeller stopped. The silence was terrifying. I tried to grip the plywood insides of the plane.

"You see, the hunters could then see me and come for what they're after."

We circled once, then twice, and we were falling.

"Are you going to start the engine soon?" I asked. "There's no game down there."

He laughed and turned the key. The engine started.

"What would you have done if it didn't start?" My head was killing me.

"Land," he said matter-of-factly.

"Where?" I looked down at the trees, rocks and hill-sides.

"We'd find a place."

We went back to the field we had left from. I got out and Eric jammed himself and his camera in the back. I don't know how he had room to take pictures but his camera rolled through most of the flight. On the film there are scenes of earth and sky rising and falling and mostly spinning. Then the earth comes closer and closer as Jimmy shows Eric how he lands in a river. On the film is the sound of Eric's voice screaming, "We're going to crash," as they hit the river-bank and bounce into the water.

They did not crash. Eric got out and filmed Jimmy as he taxied out into the river with his wheels completely under water so he could get room to take off. The plane roars out of the river with water shooting out from under its wings and it bounces over rocks along the bank before it lifts into the sky. It made a beautiful part of the story.

Like all bush pilots, Jimmy told us he was saddened by the rules and regulations of modern aviation. Later, on the way back to town, I mentioned that some of the things he does could cost him his licence.

"Nope," he said, "I don't have one."

Jimmy Anderson, survivor, with his crippled fingers, cowboy hat and wrinkled face, could walk down any street in New York or fly over any mountain in Canada and feel comfortable.

After we left him, I climbed to the top of a hill. I looked out over an area five times larger than New York City—without a house in it. Distant trees grew as thick as moss. Below me on the gravel-topped Alaska Highway, one pickup truck was heading north. It was a beautiful sight.

What's Behind Those Stories?
III: Fishing for Tales

Almost twenty-five years later the equipment has improved, but there is an amazing lack of progress in the story-gathering technique.

John McCarron and I were in Kamloops, BC, looking for stories, which means we were looking for anything that seemed interesting and would stay still long enough for us to get a picture of it. We looked at a map and saw Tranquille, which I thought was a nice name for a town. On the map it looked to be a short drive west of the Smitty's restaurant in Kamloops where we were having breakfast.

"Let's go see if life is really tranquil in Tranquille."

That is in-depth reporting, and it is with that premise in mind that we started driving west on Tranquille Road. On the way we passed a garden that had a headboard and footboard from a bed stuck in the ground. Between the two were some flowers and a sign that said Flower Bed.

"Stop, holy mackerel, what a brilliant idea," said one of us. We both wanted to take credit for seeing it first so I am not sure which of us actually said "Stop!"

It was a neat picture. It was funny. We knocked on the door. "Come on, please answer." We knocked again.

There was no one home. "Damn." It wasn't funny any more. A picture without a person telling us why and how and anything else they can think of doesn't count. Political reporters might get away with that, but not us. Strike one.

We got back in the van and continued on Tranquille Road, past forests, past fields and past the concrete foundation of a building that had been destroyed by fire.

"I wish we could use that in a story," I said. We stopped and looked and walked around and it didn't help at all. Neither of us could figure out what the building had been. Strike two.

We drove farther, up a hill and up a dusty logging road with dusty logging trucks coming down.

"This doesn't look like a tranquil place to me," said John. "In fact I don't think there is anything up here. In fact I think this is a dumb idea and if we don't find a story soon we are going to be behind schedule and if we could be fired we *would* be fired and it will be your fault."

I got out his camera and managed to get half of his head in the frame of the picture while he was still considering how nice it would be if he could punch me in the nose. I would have got more of him in the picture but he was the cameraman and I didn't want him to look like a better reporter than me or he'd have my job.

Part of my job is to complain about the pictures of the cameraman. The cameraman's job is to complain that the editor used the wrong pictures and it is both of their jobs to complain that my writing made no sense. Television is a very critical art form.

I told him not to worry, that we would find a story soon. I did this by singing a few bars from the old song about picking yourself up, dusting yourself off and starting over.

He smiled when I started singing and I thought it was my voice that was making him happy. "Be quiet," he said. "That is a nice song. And here is how it *should* sound." He put a CD into the player in his van and Diana Krall began singing the same tune.

"Okay, let's go back down the hill and find a story," I said.

Five minutes later we saw a logging truck pulled over on the side of the road. We stopped in front of it and walked back. The driver was sitting in the cab, eating a sandwich. We talked for a minute and he told us he had been driving this same road all his life. Well, that's good enough for a start on a story, I said, and John took out his camera and I began interviewing him. The gist of the conversation was: "This is a miserable job with lots of dirt and dust and I would like to do something else." Uh, oh, I thought. This is not going to be uplifting.

"Tranquille isn't any town," he said. "It's an old, abandoned nut farm where they kept the crazies and I used to ride my bike in there when I was a kid." Can't use that either; the coalition to abolish crude labels and everything else not politically correct on earth will sue us.

"That burned-out building," he explained, "was an old pig farm where I used to ride my bike when I was a kid." No kidding? A pig farm? I don't know why, but *that* sounds neat.

"And this is my birthday," he added.

Bingo! Birthdays are always special, whether you get arrested on them or celebrate. And a birthday is good enough reason to put him on television. Why not? It is better than a four-car pileup.

I wished him a happy birthday and we did a story, a profile, on the logging truck driver who has a ham and cheese sandwich that substitutes for a birthday cake. We have pictures of other logging trucks and the dust and their big tires digging their way up the hill. And we talk about the childhood of a driver who used to ride a bicycle on this same road, and the dreams and ambitions he still has to do something else with his life.

The unbelievable part of this is it works, and works so well. You get to meet a person who has dust on his face and in his hair and you join him for lunch and learn some things about him and wish him a happy birthday.

The story ends with him driving off down the road of his life with his tires throwing dirt into the air and over that picture Diana Krall sings the end of that song, about how you may be sick and tired, "but you'll be a man, my son." It may not be inspirational, but it's more honest than profiling a politician.

We should have been through now, but no. As we drove back we passed the burned-out pig farm and saw a tiny trailer parked in the middle of it. We drove in, parked in a field of weeds that had grown up where pigs were held for slaughter, and walked to the trailer. A friendly-looking couple sat on folding chairs, taking in the sun. They had come here to go gold panning, but first they had to find a stream. We wished them good luck and secretly wished we could do a story about them, but no creek, no story. We returned to the van.

"Damn," said John. The left rear tire was flat.

We could have called a tow truck, but we knew they would say, "You're *where?*"

So we got out the jack and tire iron and began trying to figure out how to put the jack together. There are courses that should be mandatory when you get a new vehicle, but they are not. After we got the jack together we tried it on three spots under the van before we found one where it could do what it was supposed to do.

So let us record this event with the camera, we said, if nothing else at least for a joke. But it was not funny, because the ground where the jack was sitting had a dip in it and we couldn't raise the jack high enough to lift the van.

The prospector and his wife came and watched, then brought a shovel so we could dig under the tire, but the ground there was made of rock and shale and would not be dug by any human. So they brought a pickaxe and we took turns trying to hack away at a spot right below the tire without impaling the tire itself. We dug, they helped, they laughed, we laughed, and John kept taking pictures, except when it was his turn to dig. He was not going to get out of working, no sir, not just so he could take pictures. So I took the camera and took very bad pictures while he dug, which I thought was a good division of labour.

Changing a flat should have taken twenty minutes. An hour later we were still trying to figure out how to get the spare out from under the van. But eventually it was done—in truth, everything eventually gets done—and we had the pictures, and so we had another story. It was not a tale of two incompetents trying to change a tire, but of a generous and friendly couple who helped. John also got a picture of them filling in the hole that we had dug out under the tire. They were good people.

That story ended with John saying, "Okay, now we'll try to find something to put on television," and over a picture of his van disappearing down a hill the voice of Diana Krall again sings that passage about picking yourself up and starting all over again. I've never met you, but thanks, Diana.

On the way back to town we stopped again at the flowerbed house on Tranquille Road, and this time a man was home.

"It was my wife who did it, and she's away for a few days," he said.

"Well, weed it out and tell us how wonderful and imaginative your wife is," we said, not having a clue what to do with the tape or any pictures that would come from it.

He weeded. He spoke. We taped. We left, and one

block away, still on Tranquille Road, we saw two girls sitting on a lawn in children's chairs, waving to passing cars.

"Stop!" one of us said.

The girls, both teenagers, had nothing else to do so they'd decided to wave at cars. And for the past week, that's what they'd been doing.

Now, that is crazy. That is also funny. And what dedication. They became their own street theatre with an interactive audience. Some drivers waved back, some honked. Some, for reasons no sane person on this planet could understand, gave them the finger. There was good, there was evil, and there was humour. It wasn't a story but John took pictures and I interviewed, and then we left.

We asked ourselves: is all this leading somewhere? We didn't know, so we had dinner, went for a walk, then went back to our hotel rooms and watched CNN, which is real news of politicians and bombings and presidents and prime ministers giving speeches. That is the big-time news with real reporters. We were just a couple of backwoods wanderers kicking up dust and meeting a few people.

The next day we went to Tranquille, the old mental institution that the logging truck driver called the nut farm. It was built as a World War I-era tuberculosis sanatorium, then was used as a mental institution in the 1950s and '60s. We looked around and experienced the eeriness of a town with streets and buildings and playgrounds but not a soul living there. "Some people say there are ghosts here," said the caretaker. And before he could finish by adding, "but that's all nonsense, of course," a story about the Ghosts of Tranquille was being born.

If you look at buildings in which many have died and many more have suffered, and if you look at empty streets on which many have walked while fighting with demons and not believe in ghosts, then you are denying your own feelings. No person can walk over a battlefield without feeling strange, as though he is not alone. No person can walk through the empty hallways of an abandoned institute for the mentally disabled without feeling the pain of others.

Those feelings are real. You don't have to prove a feeling, you sense it as clearly as your own breath. And if you feel there are ghosts in a place where there once were people then there *are* ghosts. That is a plain fact.

It does not matter if the ghosts are really speaking to us, or we are creating the whole thing in our minds, because even if they only live in our thoughts, who is to say that disproves them? Perhaps that is the way they get around. Reality be damned, when you feel you are not alone, you are not.

But we did not do an *X-Files* type story; of course not. We simply showed the place as it is, talked about its history and heard from the caretaker that some people, not him of course, believe there are ghosts there. And we looked at vacant swings moving in the breeze and at weeds growing in cracks in the sidewalks on which no one was walking. It is the kind of story that, when it is over, you don't say anything. You don't say "That was a neat story," or "That was as dumb as a rain gutter." You just don't say anything because you are thinking about some ghost somewhere, long ago.

On our way back to Kamloops, we passed a creek. We walked along it for a short while and found a man taking his dog for a walk. The man had a cane and the dog had a limp. The man had arthritis and the dog had been stepped on by a horse when it was a puppy.

A man who had trouble walking, taking a walk with a dog who had trouble walking. Even a bureaucrat would see the humanity in that. A little bit of tape and a brief interview later, and we were gone. It was time for lunch, and time to combine three oddball situations with ordinary, everyday characters into one story. The flowerbed/girls waving/dog-walking story had no beginning, no middle and no end, but it was like going to a party and meeting people who make you laugh, sigh and feel good, and you talk about them for a while afterwards.

Add to that the logging truck driver's birthday, the prospectors who helped change a tire and the ghosts of Tranquille and that is how four stories came out of two days on a brief trip to Kamloops. And I suppose finding a lesson in there isn't all that hard to do: if you want to know what is happening in politics, or about the wars of the world, you should watch CNN or the first forty-five minutes of BCTV, or read a newspaper. But if you're simply interested in real, everyday people doing real, everyday things, you don't have to look very far. And perhaps best of all, you don't need a TV or a camera to do it.

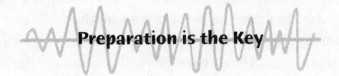

Preparation is the Key

It was hot. It was July in Vancouver and I was waiting for a cameraman to come free.

"Not yet," said Dale Hicks, whose job it is to juggle cameras. He has an impossible task because of reporters who tell him: "I need a camera *now. Right now.* I *got* to have it. If I don't have it now the story will go away and I'll get fired."

"Soon," says Dale, who used to be a reporter, before he got that Epstein-Barr illness and took off for five years to rest. During his rest he discovered golf. "Golf is better than reporting," he says. The only thing Dale needs now is more rest so he can improve his putting. But Dale also has to fulfill the wishes of the assignment editor, who says, "I need this press conference covered *now.*"

"And where would we get the camera from?" asks Dale.

That is why I was waiting for a cameraman to come free. I was on Beach Avenue in my old Honda. It has almost half a million kilometres on it and it is nicely broken in. But it doesn't have air conditioning so I had parked under a tree. And then my eyes got heavy.

And I dreamed of beautiful things. The kind of things you dream of when you are at peace with the world and you are under a shady tree. That's why God invented hot Julys and shady trees. They are medicines that take away the pains of life, like a lack of cameras.

Time passed. I only know it passed because my cell-phone was ringing and I couldn't remember where I was or why I was there.

It was Dale. Damn. Something is very wrong when work interrupts sleep.

"If you have a story, we have a camera. This will be your only chance all day." He said they had Ken Chu free for an hour between other assignments. "But if you have to hunt for something, forget it."

I opened my eyes. That is a fundamental rule of reporting. And down at the bottom of a grassy slope near a parking lot not far from the Aquatic Centre was a bunch of guys playing soccer.

"Sure, I have a story," I said. "It's a neat story. It's about soccer and I'll tell you the rest of it later."

In ten minutes Ken and I were on the edge of the field; he was taking pictures and I was praying.

"What's this about?" Ken asked.

"I don't know. Just keep shooting. Something will happen." Then I prayed some more.

I asked them if they played a lot. Yes, they did. They

were just a bunch of friends and whenever they could get lunch hours off they played soccer. They had all grown up playing soccer. Then I watched them play some more.

Well, that was something, I thought. Guys who have been playing soccer all their lives. It was not *much* of something, but somehow there might be a story in that. I was lying to myself, of course. If you have been studying the Dead Sea scrolls all your life, now *that* is something. Or if you have been collecting stamps from Tonga all your life, and you have developed pen pals so you can get the stamps, and if all the stamps are stuck to shells from sea snails, that also would be something. But playing soccer? I don't think so.

"Hey, you know something," said one of the players as he ran past me. "See those two guys?" He pointed at the two as he kept running down field. Then he shouted as he got farther away: "One is from Israel and the other is a Palestinian. And they are not shooting each other."

Thank you, story god.

"Hey, you see those two guys?" I said to Ken. "One is from Israel and the other is a Palestinian."

"How come they aren't shooting each other?" he asked.

"Pictures, my brilliant friend. Pictures!"

I felt like Steven Spielberg with an Academy Award and world peace coming from this story.

My informer ran past us again. "And I'm from Turkey and that fellow over there is from Greece."

He kept running and for some reason I was being blessed.

"Ken!" I shouted. "Those two."

119

If we could bring Greece and Turkey together, we could bring the Canadian peacekeepers home from Cyprus.

"Stop!" I shouted. Shouting was now the only way to deal with the situation, like a director yelling "Cut!" because everything is going so well he has to interfere.

"Stop playing for a second."

They did, and with the camera rolling I asked the nearest player, "Where are you from?"

"Russia."

"And you?" I asked the next.

"Hungary."

"And you?

"Czechoslovakia."

All of them started wandering over. "The Philippines." "England." "India." "Scotland." "Germany." "Wales." There were two from England and two from India. But of the sixteen guys who got together to play soccer, only one was born in Canada.

Only in Canada. Quite truly, only in Canada. There has been massive migration to the United States, but in all my years in that country I never saw so many former enemies, in fact so many cultures that normally kill each other, playing together. The only land they were fighting over was between the goalposts.

And then there was the man taking the pictures with the TV camera, who is from China, and the fellow with the microphone, who was born in New York.

This was a beautiful story. I knew it was good before I finished interviewing the players. I knew it was wonderful

Meanwhile, Chester Grant, who can find out anything about anybody at any time and who directs all the researchers and spends seven and a half hours a day on the phone, finishes a call and writes on a note: "stolen car." His notes could be used for police and court reports. They have every known fact in every case, except that no one other than himself can read them.

Chester has two passions: sitting at a desk getting information from everywhere in the world, and being on the side of a vertical rock wall trying to get three inches above where he currently is holding on without falling a long way back to the starting line. But he has done so much finger-crippling rock climbing that he can no longer hold a pen in any traditional way. His notes are not recognizable in any language. Hence he has established his own job security. His notes are the groundwork for half the stories on the news, and only he is able to read them.

"Hellonewsroom," Luizs Gaucher says into a phone. It is all one word, as is her "HellonewsroomcanIhelpyou?" A thousand times a day she says that into a phone.

"I have a problem with Tony Parsons," says the caller. "I think he's anti-union. He used to be pro-union, now he's anti-union."

"I'll give you our comment line," says Luizs, who listens to every complaint and finds old stories for callers and solves domestic problems for those who call newsrooms because they think they'll get an answer. Another line is ringing. "Can I put you on hold?"

At the end of that phone is a reporter. "I've got to talk

to that idiot in production. She doesn't know what's going on."

He didn't say hello. He didn't say who he is. He didn't say which idiot he wanted to talk to. While a third line is ringing, Luizs shouts across the newsroom, "Who in production has time to talk to an idiot reporter?"

As a fourth line is ringing she transfers the reporter to a production person who has a pencil behind each ear and a latte in one hand.

A fifth line is ringing. "Newsroom, can I put you on hold?"

"No! I am sick of being put on hold," shouts the voice on the phone. "That's the problem with our world. Everyone is put on hold."

Luizs looks at the phone board. It is lit like a Christmas tree but without any cheer. Outside of work she cooks and keeps house for her husband and kids, and her parents live in another part of her home. Her life so perfectly fits the definition of normal. But in the newsroom, she is the underpaid queenpin, tougher than an old cowboy, who deals with one problem after another, after another. If she were a juggler there would be a circle of complaints and news tips circling over her head. Watching her can exhaust you.

These phones don't stop day or night. After Luizs leaves—and she walks five miles every day to get home in any weather, including rain and snow, just to get the phone calls out of her head—then Gerry takes over. Gerry O'Hagan wears a baseball cap and tries to watch hockey games while listening to police and fire calls and talking to callers who remember there was some medicine mentioned somewhere on some show and they aren't sure what it does but could he tell them about it and also where to get it and how much does it cost, and what does he think is wrong with them? Gerry works harder and knows more than the big shot reporters who only have to deal with one subject at a time, and always have researchers to help them.

"Can't you find enough time to talk to me?" says the voice on the phone. "Or am I not important enough? That's the problem, right? I'm not—"

"Excuse me, sir," says Luizs, "I have to put you on hold."

A sixth line is ringing.

"Hello. Listen, I can only talk for a second. You know the car that went into the ditch this morning? It was a kid driving it."

"Clive!" Luizs covers the mouthpiece and shouts, "Clive! That car this morning. It was a kid driving. I've got somebody here."

Clive Jackson looks around the room. There are no reporters in the newsroom. They are all out doing stories.

Clive was once a reporter on Fleet Street in London, where he fell in love with the smell of hot, hard news. He also worked as a hotel bellhop in Los Angeles, where he learned to deal with most of the oddball people who walk the earth. Now he is the assignment editor, the man who runs the day-to-day operation and decides what will be covered and what will not and how to stretch resources that never stretch far enough.

He learned his skills of sniffing out potential stories and sending reporters out to bring them in under the legendary Keith Bradbury, who was assignment editor and then news director through most of BCTV's time on this planet. Bradbury at work made a pit bull seem timid. No reporter called him more than once in his or her working career to say that the interviewee had refused to be interviewed, or that the fire really wasn't as bad as reported earlier, or that the story was too hard or too far or too miserable or that they had missed the boat or plane or train.

On the phone you would hear the distant thunder rumbling. Then, like a hurricane that obliterates everything in its way, would come Bradbury's voice: "GO BACK AND GET THE F%$#@ING STORY. AND DON'T COME BACK UNTIL YOU DO!!!" It was encouragement like that which created endless prize-winning stories and pushed BCTV to unprecedented levels of viewership. Bradbury was like a drill sergeant in basic training. He got you to do things you never thought you could do, or would do, or would dare to do. And then you swore if you ever were in his position you would be different.

Clive felt the thunder, and since then has tried the bellhop's secrets for success: smile, and con them into doing what you want done.

"Hello, this is Clive Jackson," he says into the phone to the person who says a kid was driving the car. "You could be a hero to us if you would tell us more."

The caller tells him the driver was a juvenile. But the

caller will not tell his own name and will not be interviewed and wants to hang up.

"Wait. We need people like you. We need people who are brave, who will stand up and say things. Believe me, only you can help us."

"Sorry, fella. Got to go."

He hangs up and Clive curses. He phones a reporter and pulls her off the story she is doing and tells her to find out if this dead driver was really a juvenile in a stolen car. "Only you can do this," says Clive.

Chester looks up from his notes and says he can only confirm it was a stolen car. He has no information on the juvenile part.

There is another meeting. This time the news director, Steve Wyatt, is involved. Steve was once told by management at BCTV that he was not good enough to be a reporter. He just didn't have what it took, they said. He left and went to Toronto and worked his way up through the networks, slugging it out with other reporters and then with other assignment editors and then with other news directors. Each time he came out on top. A dozen years later he came back to Vancouver as news director of CKVU, which under his leadership became BCTV's main competition. He did so well that management at BCTV said they had to have someone like him at the helm. "See if we can lure him back. We can't afford to have him with the competition."

Steve is now the chief guy in the newsroom. He will be consulted and will make some very expensive decisions. If the driver was a juvenile, the entire show will be remade.

There will be stories on other juveniles who have stolen cars. Lawyers and police will be interviewed. The lead story will go long and it will go live from the scene. Other stories that have been worked on will be dropped. Clive will have to pull several other reporters off stories that are sure things and have them work on assorted juvenile delinquency stories.

If we are the only station with the story, our ratings will go up. That allows us to raise advertising rates. That is how the station makes enough money to pay its employees. If the story is false, and by spending time on it we lose other important stories of the day, which other stations may have, then ratings will fall. You are the news director, make up your mind. And be quick.

"Go for it," Steve says.

Clive's stomach starts to turn. Who gets pulled off their stories? What do they sacrifice? Whom does he have to fight with on the phone, telling him that the story he was earlier encouraged to get is now dead, and to forget the work of the last four hours and start again on something new? And by the way, you only have ninety minutes to do it.

He starts. The phone call is nothing you want to repeat at home.

"Yes, I mean it."

Profanity from the other end.

"But we've got to do it."

More profanity.

"You are the only one who can do it."

"%$#&%$!!!" from the reporter. Then, "Okay. Where do you want me to go?"

For the next thirty minutes, two shows are being planned. If it is a dead juvenile car thief it will be a tragedy and an amazing newscast with only one problem.

"How can we get all this together in an hour?" says Clive, who will be late for dinner—again. "If it is not true, pray we will have enough time to go back to plan A, which is not a bad show."

There is no sense in getting overly dramatic about this. It is a working day and Clive is lucky so far. The first reporter he asked to check it out has a contact with the police and calls back in half an hour. It was a stolen car. But it was only someone who *looks* young. He is over eighteen. Probably the person who called in thought he looked like a juvenile. But no, he is not a juvenile.

"It's a voice-over," says Clive.

The translation of that is the car in the ditch is now a story that will be told in under twenty seconds. There will be pictures of the car being pulled out of the ditch and Tony will read a script that says the driver of a stolen car was killed early this morning when the car flipped over and rolled into a water-filled ditch in Surrey, BC. Police say they are waiting for an autopsy, but early indications are the driver had been drinking.

"Now, where do I put it?" says Randy McHale.

Randy used to sell hot tubs, but he wanted to be a reporter so he went to university and got a master's degree in journalism, which is very hard to do. Then he got a job as a reporter with BCTV. On his first story he found he hated reporting. Randy is brilliant, probably one of the best, fastest and most thoughtful writers in the country. He can describe a tragedy in a way that tells the story but doesn't offend or hurt even those who are suffering. Randy decided he wanted to write, so long as he didn't have to interview people. Before his first year with the TV station was over, he moved inside behind a typewriter and began composing virtually every word that Tony Parsons said. That was more than twenty years ago.

Randy was very happy with his job and he was doing it very well, so he was promoted to something else. He was given the much harder job of lining up the show. Most in this business considered the lineup editor as the most crucial part of television. How do you put the stories of the day, which often have nothing to do with each other, into some kind of order that will seem to make sense? How do you juggle murders with stories of a child's first day in kindergarten? And how do you do that when the stories are constantly changing in size and content? How do you inform without offending?

Where do the two sentences about the car in the ditch go? Not at the end of a package because it is depressing without much redeeming value. Not at the beginning because it is not strong enough. Not high in the show because of its decreased importance. Not at the end because that is where lighter stories go.

The car in the ditch is squeezed between the story about new provincial insurance rates and a consumer item about tire safety.

At 6:25 p.m. in the control room where the director is

saying "Camera one, up on Tony," a production assistant keeps a second-by-second count of the length of the show.

"We are twenty seconds over," she says.

Tim Perry, who now writes most of the witty lines that the anchors read, is behind the director. After each reporter finishes their story they call Tim, who has replaced Randy as the main writer on the News Hour. Every day I say something like: "Tim, this is about a blind dog and a couple of people who take care of him and they've had him for a long time and the dog's not very big and he's really old and I've got to get going, Okay?"

I don't have time to say any more, because like all reporters I have to drive to the station and worry about how the story is coming together, and besides, the introduction is Tim's problem. But with those bits of information he writes something that makes Tony Parsons sound compassionate and the reporter, me, look good. He writes, "Love can be expressed in many ways. But caring for something that can't see you and can't respond to you, especially when the object of the love was included in your family only because you wanted to care for it, is more love than most are willing to give."

He writes this after he has crafted an introduction to a murder story, and before he has to listen to a summary of a business problem and write three sentences that encapsulate how the economy is behaving in relation to the stock market. He writes on thirty subjects a day, and between heavy subjects he rests his mind by working out a baseball schedule for the office team. Now he must decide what gets dropped.

Every story is important. He has already taken twenty seconds out of the weather forecast and twenty more out of sports. He must trim fat from a body that has none.

"Drop the car in the ditch," he says.

Downstairs in the roll-to-air room where the tapes are put into a machine that sends them out on the air, the video cassette with the pictures of the car getting pulled out of the ditch is slid out of the lineup and put back on a shelf. And without a blink, the teleprompter moves on to the next story. Television is like life. Don't ever count on even the smallest things going the way you plan.

Thursday, May 18, 2000

I've had worse days. There was the time I asked for a raise from a radio station and they fired me. But this was also the best of days because the story god smiled at me. On the other hand, maybe he was laughing.

It started with cornmeal porridge. My wife and I began eating that when we lived in the southern US and got grits with every meal. Grits is cornmeal so thick you can leave your spoon standing in it like the mast of a ship. Why would you leave your spoon like that? Well, because there are too many rules in the world, too much of what you *should* do, and if you don't do something crazy once in a while you get to be legally, properly, politely dulled to death. It is good to start breaking the rules early, like at breakfast.

Grits often comes with catfish, which is sort of the salmon of the South. The problem is that the world is running out of salmon because of over-fishing and a changing environment. However, the world is never going to run out of catfish because they are bottom-feeding swill-eaters that turn worms and gunk into rich, tasty flesh. That is a great evolutionary move of self-preservation on their part. They gave up chasing their food like other fish, and by eating stuff other fish leave behind they improved their odds of not being eaten by us.

"You're not going to eat a bottom eater, are you? Yuck."

Unless of course you live in the South, where catfish and grits is often chosen over burgers and fries.

But my wife and I were not discussing catfish at breakfast. We had a bigger issue, which was the cornmeal. She said I had made it lumpy.

"What's wrong with lumpy cornmeal? It helps your spoon stand up," I said.

"It tastes like balls of uncooked grits," she said as she rolled yellow marbles out of the porridge.

Like most families, we start the morning discussing badly stirred cornmeal or burned toast while dreaming of sitting by the bayou watching catfish jumping out of the water. They breathe air, you know, so they have to come up every few minutes and the thing you do in the South is lounge with your friends by the edge of a backwater and say, "Look, there's another catfish."

In the North, on the other hand, we sit in the cafeteria and say, "Did you see *Ally McBeal* last night?"

"Yeah. But do you think the rain's going to stop soon?"

It is rich thoughts like those that stimulate our minds.

Anyway, after breakfast I took my wife to the dentist and

while she was in the chair I went for a walk around the neighbourhood. I was only one block from a busy part of central Lonsdale in North Vancouver, passing the back of an apartment house, when I saw a white-haired man standing with an easel on a tiny first-floor balcony painting a picture of a sailing ship.

"Thank you, story god," I whispered.

The balcony looked out onto a solid asphalt parking lot with half a dozen dumpsters. What a great contrast to sailing ships. Thank you again, story god.

I said hello to the artist and told him the painting looked wonderful. He said there were still some ships like this down in the harbour when he was a boy. Thank you, thank you, story god. It is my mantra. You must never forget to thank the story god or you will be cut off.

Then the friendly, gentle old artist said, and I am quoting him directly, "When I was young you could lay down on Georgia Street and go to sleep."

Where's the cameraman? Why aren't these words being recorded?

We talked more and the old man told me how he remembered when this area—and he waved his hand over the parking lot—was all forest.

This is a gold mine of history and humanity.

I told him where I was from and asked if I could come back with someone and take his picture.

"Sure," he said, "that would be fun."

His white-haired wife pushed open the sliding door to the balcony and I thought, this is even better, an enduring love story.

He introduced me. She said, and I'm quoting her directly because there are things you don't forget, "We don't want
any goddamn photographers around here."

"But he wants to put me in the newspaper," the fellow
said.

That was quaint to hear. He is from the generation that
doesn't think television is the source of all things. He thinks
of unmoving photographs and the written word.

"We don't want any goddamn picture in the newspaper," said his wife. "They will cut off our cheques."

"No, they won't," said the man.

Uh oh, was my immediate thought.

"No they won't," I said, trying to sound positive.

"You don't know nothing," she said to me. Then she
said to her husband, "If you are in the newspaper they will
cut off our pension cheques."

"No, I guarantee they won't," I said.

"You can't guarantee anything!" she shouted at me.

Whoops, I thought. This is not the best of all possible
worlds. I did not know if she was on medication that she had
forgotten to take, or if she had been this pleasant all of their
married life.

I watched the two of them arguing on the balcony about
being in the newspaper or on TV and losing or not losing
their pension cheques and I whispered "Good luck" to the
man who did not hear me and I walked away.

Okay, story god. You've had your fun. Now you owe me
one.

An hour later, after my wife had explained how the

dentist told her that her teeth are in good shape, except for the expensive work that has to be done, I was out working with cameraman John McCarron. We were driving along Powell Street when I saw a man through the window of the Able Moving Company. He had his feet up on a desk. Now there is someone who knows how to relax. "Stop," I said.

While John got his camera gear ready I went inside. It was a beautiful sight. The man was a rustic picture of rest: feet up, hands behind his head, a desk piled with papers, an ashtray piled with ashes. I had been looking for a character and now he was sitting right in front of me.

"You sure know how to relax," I said.

"Bored," he said. "The moving business can be boring."

I told him who I was and he said he knew. He watched the show. Then he said, "Look at this."

He handed me what looked like a five-pin bowling ball, except it was silver. It was solid and heavy.

"That's how bored I am," he said. "That's all from the aluminum foil in cigarette packs."

He took a pack from his pocket and removed the slip of foil that is wrapped around the cigarettes inside. The foil is lined with paper. He separated the two with his fingernail. The foil was thinner than a hair and weighed nothing.

"I've rolled those together to make the ball," he said.

"There must be five or ten thousand packs in there," I said.

"Yup, about that."

Then he showed me a second ball that was half the size of the first.

"I'm working on that one."

"Thank you, story god," I said in the back of my head.

"Can we take a picture of this and you?" I asked.

It was wonderful. A character who smokes and when people saw what he was doing it might turn them off smoking. At the very least they would remember him. I was so happy I was giddy.

"No, no one ever takes my picture."

"But—"

"No one."

"But you would be wonderful," I tried.

"No."

"You could help people stop smoking."

"No."

"We'll just show the ball and you tell us how you made it."

"No. No one ever takes my picture, you can ask my wife."

I was thinking, I don't want to ask your wife. But what I said was, "I guess you mean no."

"You got it."

I left cursing the story god.

"This is not going to be a good day," I said to John.

We continued down the street past Oppenheimer Park, which is the lungs of Skid Road. It once was a fancy park. After that, during World War II, it held Japanese-Canadians in temporary detention before they were sent to camps in the BC Interior. Now most of its clients stretch out on the grass between bottles of wine and food lines. It is an interesting place.

140

Once I did a story here about old Japanese folks playing an Oriental form of croquet. These were really good and strong people who had their homes taken away from them and survived the detention camps during the war, and yet they still say Canada is their home and they never have a bad word for it. They still come to this park because this area was once Japan Town and a Japanese Buddhist monastery is across the street. And this is the park where they have always played their game with wooden mallets hitting the balls across the worn-out grass. They wear bright, fresh, crisp clothing and bow to each other while around them are men and women, some of whom have seen the inside of the jail and drunk tank many times.

And yet these frail old players have never had a ball stolen or been harassed or even been spoken to badly by the others in the park. The story had two entirely different and fascinating styles of lives crossing back and forth without harming each other. It is quite possible this could only happen in Canada.

And there was a time when I did an endless series on drugs and drug dealing, and at that time the drug dealers had largely taken over Oppenheimer Park. That was in the early '90s and I did story after story on how the park was dying. We shot several of the stories from hiding places inside apartments across the street from the park, but I did not know that at the same time the police were doing their own surveillance from the roofs of the apartment buildings. One day while I was doing an on-camera essay on how bad drugs are, the plainclothes police of the drug squad burst out of a half-dozen unmarked cars and tackled drug dealers right behind me. Thank you, story god.

Wham, one got tackled on camera. Slam, two were tackled. Karl Casselman, a cameraman with more energy than most gazelles, was running after one takedown after another. Several guys tried to throw the drugs out of their pockets as they ran and were chased by police in what looked like a football game, except this was real life. Karl got incredible pictures, and this was years before all those real-life police shows came on TV.

Maybe this day, the 18th of May, would be another exciting day here. In the park we saw a guy who obviously hadn't changed his clothes, combed his hair or bathed since Christmas. But he was sitting at a picnic table and on it he was setting up a chessboard. And he had all the pieces in the right places.

I had learned to play chess in Germany when I was a teenager. I learned from a Russian fellow named Alex, who had escaped with his mother and older brother across a frontier of barbed wire and searchlights. They had crawled on their bellies through dark nights and slept in the grass of farm fields during the day. My chess teacher was no softy. Every time I see a chess game I get flashbacks of the years I spent in Germany. It was the most influential time of my life. It probably saved my life.

Before I went there I was a fourteen-year-old street urchin, living with my mother and skipping school a lot. She had left a violent, drunken husband when I was seven and I grew up as an original latchkey kid. My mother went to work before I woke in the morning and she didn't get home until long after dark.

As a result I spent a lot of time on the street and thought I could pretty nearly take on any kid in my neighbourhood, or any other neighbourhood.

"He's got no father, he must be tough." I don't know what that had to do with reality, but I heard it a lot so I made it come true.

Then when I was fourteen and failing every subject in school, including gym, my mother came home from work one night and said, "Do you want to go to Germany?"

"Sure," I said. "Where's Germany?"

Two weeks later we were in Munich. It was 1958 and every other block in the city was piled high with the bombed-out rubble of buildings. It had been thirteen years since the war ended, but it looked as though the fighting had taken place a week earlier. The apartment house we moved into had machine-gun bullet holes across the front of it. Many of the men I saw were missing arms and legs. The ones without legs pushed themselves along on wooden boards that were nailed together and mounted on tiny wheels, so that the men moved about a few inches above the ground. The ones who were missing both arms and legs went nowhere.

My mother was working for Radio Free Europe. She was a teletype operator, and they needed a teletype operator in Munich and they needed her quickly. She was an exceptional typist who could type in any language without having a clue what she was sending, and she was so fast she could take dictation on a keyboard.

This was when the Cold War was bubbling hot. The front of the radio station had tank traps protecting it and guards with Tommy guns walked the perimeter of the building. One day a Bulgarian spy sneaked into the cafeteria in the station and poured cyanide in all the salt shakers. This was when cholesterol was unknown and everyone ate bacon and eggs for breakfast and everyone used salt. A confession about the cyanide was beaten out of the spy by another spy minutes before breakfast time and the good spy crashed through the doors of the cafeteria screaming, "Stop! Stop! Drop your forks! Don't move!"

This information had to be sent back to Radio Free Europe headquarters in New York and it was my mother who was the messenger sitting at the keyboard.

"My hands froze," she told me. She also ate in the cafeteria.

Radio Free Europe was a secret arm of the CIA, but that was so secret we didn't even talk about it at home. The apartment house we lived in was filled with employees of the station. There were engineers on the top floor, all of whom had the same hobby: short-wave radio. There were enough antennas on that roof to electrocute people in the basement if it ever got hit by lightning. But all the engineers said they used their radios just to call friends in South America. Yeah, sure.

There were only two American families in the building. The others were refugees from behind the Iron Curtain, and the first girlfriend I had was a Hungarian who lived on the fourth floor. When she was twelve she had stood in the streets of Budapest and thrown gasoline-filled bottles at Russian tanks. I no longer thought I was so tough.

One day I wandered far from Munich on my bike. I was left alone a great deal there and explored many things. On this day I went to Dachau. That was before it was turned into a park. There was an open gate topped with barbed wire and I walked through it and in front of me were row after row of ovens. Underneath them were mounds of ashes with bits of bones sticking out. I put my head inside one of the ovens. It was long, like a tunnel, and I put my hands down to support myself and they disappeared under more ashes.

Then I went into a building in which there was a huge black box like a vault, one of the gas chambers. It was big enough to hold maybe fifty or sixty people. I could see where fingers had gouged holes into the walls. I was alone. But I was not alone.

There were more buildings, many buildings. Inside some were rows of wooden beds stacked three high. There were no windows.

Something happened to me that day, thirteen years after the ovens had gone cold and the gas into the black boxes was shut off. I do not know what happened, but no feeling, no sight, no thought has ever been the same.

Some have said what happened there during the war did not happen. They are fools, not worthy of contempt. Many have said never again. But it has happened again in Cambodia and in Africa and in the Balkans.

As a species we luckily have done some wonderful things; it helps to balance out how bad we can be.

It was in Germany that I saw the *Diary of Anne Frank*, in German. And I waited in the rain with thousands of others who wanted to see it. I learned how a nation got a sick, horrid feeling in its stomach when it sobered up from its drunken power binge and realized what it had done. And I learned how a nation can humble itself and say it is sorry and try to fix things.

I am not Jewish. I did not have a relative die in a concentration camp. I am not German. I had no relatives who said they did not know what was happening. I only know that living there when I did, I learned to feel the horror and the humanity and the hope of the victims of both sides. So when I see a chess game it means more than who is winning or what moves they are making. And here was a fellow in Oppenheimer Park who looked like he had crawled out of a dumpster and he was about to play. Once before I had covered a chess tournament—in Robson Square, and there was a Harley Davidson parked outside and a Hell's Angel playing inside. What a story. If the story god was with us we might have the same now.

"You looking for a partner?" I said to the chessman.

He took a drag on his marijuana cigarette. Then before the smoke came out of his lungs he took another drag.

He looked up at me. "How do you play this f***ing game?" he asked.

"You have all the pieces right," I said.

He took another drag. "Well, we all make mistakes," he said.

Well, story god. It is time we had a little talk.

We got back into the van and John said, "Look at that. The cheapest coffee in town." He was pointing to a sign across the street: Coffee 50 cents.

Now that would be a good story. We got out of the van again. Inside the diner we asked the waitress how she could sell coffee for fifty cents. She was a new immigrant, working very hard, and she was very tired.

"You want coffee?" she said.

"No, we want to know how you can sell coffee for fifty cents."

"You want coffee or you no want coffee?" She picked up two paper cups.

"No, we want to know how you do this."

"You no want coffee?" She had a blank, confused look on a very tired face.

"No, what we want to know is . . ." But I knew we would not learn what we wanted to know.

She put down the paper cups and shook her head, figuring we had come from the park across the street and we were too stupid to know what we wanted. We left.

There are times when I have serious talks with the deity of stories, and this was one of them. I stared out the windshield and said, "Please."

Cameramen are at a premium and they do two and sometimes three stories in a day with reporters, plus there are always press conferences they have to squeeze in or simply hare-brained ideas they have to cover from producers who sit inside all day and think big thoughts.

"Could you," a producer will say over the telephone to

a cameraman, "get a picture of a bus wheel going through a puddle with some pedestrians walking by? I have a vision of a segment on the ideal height of curbs."

Producers are overpaid. Plus the cameraman knows it hasn't rained for three days. But he will still get that phone call because the producer has a "vision." And in the office they are looking at the clock and saying, "If McCardell doesn't tell us soon that he has something, we are going to pull that camera, because we know he is wasting time drinking coffee and fooling around."

I spoke again to the story god: "Help."

We drove to Queen Elizabeth Park, which is one of my favourite places for finding things to put on TV. The reason is people go to parks to do something, and Queen Elizabeth has a great mix of people. On one side of the park are squat, dull-coloured, low-income housing projects, and on the other side are top-of-the-scale, individually landscaped, mega-sized houses belonging to the well paid. Lawn bowlers with manicured nails mixing with kids stealing golf balls, that is the human beauty of Queen Elizabeth Park.

The stories that have come out of the park are legendary, at least to my way of thinking. There were the Irish nuns who came to see the view but the smog was so heavy we had to show them postcards of what it was supposed to look like. And there are the tourists who have their pictures taken by the clock at the top of the park. They don't know why they do it, but one said, "At least I'll know what time I took the picture."

And there was the woman sewing up the holes in a

sweater her mother had worn, and now her mother was dead and the woman wanted to wear the sweater. And there was the boy walking his pet rabbit, which did not want to walk, so they both stood still and became a very touching picture and story.

There were several stories on the Tai Chi people who come in the mornings near the upper parking lot. Hundreds at the same time do the slow dance of health, along with those practising ballroom dancing without music.

They did not have to talk. We just had to watch.

And today, there was a story looking me straight in the face. Four teenage girls were playing cards and laughing and giggling. Well, that is good enough. Girls don't often play cards, it is just not what they do and anything out of the ordinary is by my definition fascinating. I said hello and asked if they were playing rummy or poker and they said they weren't really playing, they were just looking at the cards. It was a deck that had pictures of all-star wrestlers with greased skin and pumped-up muscles. The wrestlers were posing, they were tangled up with each other and they were all huge.

I looked up. Thank you.

"But we don't want to be on TV."

"What?"

"It would be too embarrassing."

"We won't embarrass you," I said. "We just want to see the cards."

"No, we couldn't."

"You could."

"No, we couldn't. People would laugh."

"No they won't," I lied. "Well, yes they will." I decided to try honesty.

"See, you know it too."

They packed up their cards.

Now, I have seen some terrible things during my years of police reporting. But at that moment the girls packing up their cards was a tearful sight. I thought of saying, "Please." I thought of giving up the last of my dignity and begging, but I have shoes older than these kids. And besides, by now they were too far away to hear. Three and a half hours had passed since John and I met. I was thinking that if I was at all competent we could have filmed *Ben Hur* in that time. I was dejected. I cannot do this job, I thought. I don't know why I try to get a story every day; it is impossible and I should go to work in a car wash. I am not really going to have an anxiety attack, I just look that way.

We drove around to the other side of the parking lot and John saw a bride and groom getting out of a car. This is not unusual in Queen Elizabeth Park since half the wedding pictures in Vancouver have the same setting in the rock quarry. One Saturday I took a still picture looking down into the quarry and it shows seven different wedding couples, each carefully manoeuvred by the photographers so each looks as though they are the only couple in love in this setting in the world.

John said we could follow this couple and do something on them, and when I looked around I saw the groom in a tuxedo putting money in the parking meter. That is funny, because it is out of context. But then I see his face and he does not look like he is enjoying this particular day. This groom has a frown that looks more like he is heading to a marriage counsellor than a wedding photographer. No, it won't work, I said. And I feared that in my present mood I could have seen Mount Baker exploding and felt the great quake shaking under our feet and met a beggar who found a lottery ticket worth $10 million, and I would say, "Nah, it's not going to work. Forget it."

We went to the top of the park where we could look down on the old rock quarry where all the wedding pictures are taken, and we saw that same wedding couple. John took a picture of them, but I admitted to him that I didn't have a clue what to do with it. John got less than ten seconds of tape shot before we heard a gardener yelling at the wedding photographer to get out of the flowerbed. The photographer had to move the bride and groom to another setting, and the spot he picked was the only place we could not see from up here. I should have expected this.

At the same time, two women sat down on a bench near us and I asked them if they came here to watch the wedding couples. No, they said, and I thought: Of course not, why would anyone say yes to anything I ask? This is a day when nothing is going to work.

They said it was their first time here, they were from Calgary. I asked if catching a glimpse of that bride before she disappeared reminded them of their weddings. They were sweet women. One told me, while the camera was on her, that she and her husband had had no money when they married and that she had always wished she could have had a real wedding dress like that one down below. But she had been married now for forty-one years and marriages are not made by a dress.

Oh, thank you.

And the other woman said she was a new immigrant when she met her husband in Canada and her mother sewed her dress by hand, but it was a practical dress that she could wear many times. She too was still married after forty years.

Thank you, again.

Then they said they were with the German-Canadian choir from Calgary.

What?! My mind is spinning. My heart is starting to work again. "Would you sing something?"

"Oh, no. We couldn't."

"Please. *Bitte*." Which is German for "please."

"Okay, what?"

"A wedding song."

"We don't know any."

"A love song. Any song. Just sing."

And they began together, singing in German a children's song about walking through a park in May and smelling the flowers.

Oh, story god, I owe you big time.

After one chorus they laughed, we thanked them, and they were gone to rejoin their group.

John took a few more pictures of people walking through the park, including an elderly couple holding hands.

We had spent four hours and fifteen minutes driving, hauling out the camera, asking questions, getting disappointed, wishing, hoping, praying and swallowing frustration to get seven minutes and twelve seconds of tape.

Two hours after we left the park there was a story on television about a bride and groom having their wedding pictures taken. Unknown to them there were others at their ceremony, including a couple of women reminiscing about their weddings, people strolling through the park, and a beautiful elderly couple still holding hands after a lifetime together. You look at their wrinkled fingers locked together and you think there is still hope, even with all the idiocy in the world. And the couple getting their wedding pictures taken may have heard some sweet music coming from an unknown place above them in an unknown language.

A German friend of mine, Gunther Blasig, who grew up during the war and escaped from East Germany while it was under Russian occupation, was at home in Maple Ridge watching the story. Later he told me he had not heard that song for fifty years and that he had sung along with the women on the television.

It really wasn't a bad day after all.

Help from an Angel

This is another story about John McCarron, the cameraman who shot the German singers. It is a story that will tell you it is not always easy to live. John will tell you sometimes life is so hard that you wish yourself to die, except you can't do that, only because it is impossible. And besides, there are others who wish you wouldn't die.

For most of John's life he went to work, rode his mountain bike after work, went to church with his wife Pat and their three daughters, and worried about his mortgage. Then one day a cop came to his door. He told John he had some bad news. His youngest daughter Christa, nineteen years old, had been killed in a car crash while driving up to Simon Fraser University. Whatever the cop said after that, whatever words of comfort he tried to give, were not heard. John only heard the words that are unbearable to hear. "Your daughter is dead."

The hell of shock and denial and depression that John and Pat and their other daughters, Melanie and Julie, lived in is unimaginable except by the few who have also been there. There is no pain worse than losing a child. There is no argument about that. It is not supposed to happen. That is not the natural order. You hear that over and over and it is true.

Go back to work? Not likely. Your mind is not on work, or eating or sleeping or washing a car or riding a bike. You are numb. You are dead, except you are still breathing.

But eventually, because there is a need for an income and because you are told you must go back to work or go crazy, you do. And the world is a blur. Only habit gets you through the first week and the second. If it wasn't for the remote control function of the brain you would just sit and stare. And even while working, the feelings that have no adequate descriptions become overwhelming and you pull over to the side of the road and grip the steering wheel tight enough to break it off. Tears are uncontrollable. They drip off your lips and chin onto your shirt.

I sat alongside him, and I wanted to say something that would help. But there was nothing. And then time passed, and we went on looking for something uplifting. Something that would make people feel good and laugh at the end of the news that night.

"Do you mind if in a little while we go to the cemetery?" he said. "After we find something, of course," he added, trying to smile, trying to put lightness back into the blackness of the day.

But this was not an easy day to find something. Some

days are like that. Some days, regardless of my mood or the cameraman's mood, there just is nothing that we see. We rely on luck, hunches, determination, intuition. I make wishes when we go over railroad tracks. Sometimes that works. I squeeze lucky rocks together and keep looking out the windshield. That works sometimes. But some days nothing works. Block after block and back lane after back lane, there is nothing. There is almost no one out and those whom we find either don't speak a language I can understand or are late for an appointment and are just leaving. "Sorry. Must go. Come back tomorrow."

An hour passed, an hour and a half, two hours, two and a half hours of weaving up and down streets. John wanted to work and he wanted to visit his daughter's grave. I wanted to work, and I wanted him to visit his daughter. And while we looked for something to do a story about, we talked about life after death. We talked of dreams and coincidences that make you say, maybe it is true. We talked of spirits while we looked for something in breathing flesh and blood. It is probably easy to explain, but with each turn we were getting closer to Vancouver's Mountain View Cemetery. We were on 33rd Avenue, only one block from his daughter's grave, when suddenly, "Stop! There it is." There is no doubt when you see it, and there we saw it.

Four kids were bowling on the front concrete walkway of their house. They were using a basketball and the pins were big pop bottles half-filled with water. Wham, a strike. Smack me on the side of my head, but doesn't that look beautiful. When you mix people of any age with inventiveness of any description you have something that is wonderful and makes you happy, and most of all is good for television.

"Stop!" I said again.

"I am stopped, you idiot," said John. "You might try moving."

He was already getting out of the van while I was still mesmerized by the kids. It doesn't take much to get my interest and in my mind I was not seeing kids bowling, but kids making a summer camp, kids playing without video games and without adults telling them what to do. I was seeing my own childhood, which, except for when I was sleeping, was lived almost entirely outdoors on concrete. I was seeing something that was warming my heart, and therefore it had a good chance of warming the hearts of those who would spend a few minutes watching the end of the news.

I was also watching John, who was already taking pictures while I was still sitting like a slug in the front seat of his van. Move, Michael.

As it turned out there were two families living side by side. The parents are from India, the kids were born here. And these kids who grew up speaking Punjabi in their kitchen and English on the street were making up their own games from what they had seen on television and heard about in school. After the bowling they showed us the fishing hole they had made out of a plastic wading pool. They put nuts and bolts in the water and tried to catch them with safety pins tied to pieces of string. To make the water dark so they couldn't see the steel fish they added soy sauce. An adult would say, don't do that, it's messy.

They were Tom Sawyers, all six and seven and eight years of them, who ate curry and played on a street in Canada instead of the Mississippi River. But they had Tom's imagination, creating a world that suited them just fine. And they showed us a clubhouse that they had built in their backyard and the rules were no swearing and to be nice to each other. John took pictures of them laughing and giggling and being proud of their accomplishments. He took pictures of their beaming faces and their homemade toys.

Oh, God. This is the kind of story that I pray for and here it was. The kids' parents came out and the kids explained what was happening and everyone was happy. We finished and got back into the van and John took the tape out of the camera and gave it to me.

And then he drove to the cemetery and stood over his daughter's grave. He knelt and brushed some dirt away from the plate with her name and picture on it and straightened some flowers.

"I think it was Christa who gave us the story," I said.

He smiled, as much as any father whose daughter is dead can smile. And he smiled as much as any father can smile when he hears that his daughter, whom he is so proud of, has done something good and has helped others.

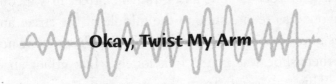

Okay, Twist My Arm

M any executives who run big successful companies and get all the recognition are basically idiots. Premiers and prime ministers are examples. If they were responsible for their own decisions their companies would soon be small and they would have to go back to work on the greenchain. Luckily they have advisors and support staff who are sharp and stay up late working on ideas. These bright young lights have ambitions to shine so that they can become executives themselves. They see the advantages: less work and better pay.

Anyway, on the day of the Shoe-in-the-Middle-of-the-Street story I was a perfect executive. I was super stupid.

I have done roughly seven thousand stories for television. A few have gotten significant mention, like chasing down a litterbug, and the series that went on for two years about mental health and the homeless. But you wouldn't believe how many people have said, "Hey, that shoe in the middle of the street, now *that* was a story."

It was nothing but an essay on a shoe under the wheels of traffic at 16th Avenue and Granville Street in Vancouver. Everyone has seen a shoe in the middle of the street and it raises questions: how did it get there? Didn't someone notice that their shoe was gone? Is it lonely? Talk about an easy task. This was a gift from the story god. And its biggest advantage was it was there, right in front of us as we drove along Granville Street.

"Hey, look at that, a shoe in the middle of the street," said Mike Timbrell, a cameraman who was born the year I got my first union card. "Let's do that."

"No," I said.

"What do you mean 'No'"? he said, looking at me like I was an idiot.

"No. I don't want to do a story about a shoe in the middle of the street."

"Why?"

"There might be someone's foot in it," I said.

"Are you nuts?" he said. "It's just a shoe. Someone lost it."

There is a difference between growing up in Coquitlam, with grass in the front yard, and growing up in New York, with grass in the air. Mike heard about the exploits of hockey players getting even with other teams by beating them. I heard about mobsters settling scores by cutting off fingers, hands and, occasionally, feet. The only thing worse than cutting off someone's feet was sticking them in wet concrete, waiting a short while and then tossing the person and the feet into the East River. To me a shoe in the middle of the street meant an unpleasant time the night before, so I said no.

We drove on, looking at cats trying to get into garbage cans, but that did not work. And we looked at a fellow selling ice cream from a truck who hated that stupid music that goes with all ice cream trucks. But he was not a happy soul so we did not do a story about him. We looked at many things, each one forgotten the moment we left it.

"How about the shoe?" Mike asked.

"No, it's stupid," I said. "There's no story to it. It's only a shoe, and besides," since I was running out of reasons not to do it, "I don't want to."

We checked more alleys and we talked to more people and nothing worked.

"The shoe?" he said.

"No."

More driving. More stopping and more talking to people. And nothing worked.

This time Mike just looked at me and raised his eyebrows.

"Okay," I said reluctantly. "We'll do the stupid shoe, but it won't work, and besides, if there's a foot in it we have to call the police and I want to do a nice story."

We headed back toward the shoe. We had to go from downtown Vancouver and even though I was hoping it would be gone by the time we got there, there it was. It had moved a bit, but it was still in the street defying tons of steel and rubber.

CHASING THE STORY GOD

Mike started taking pictures of it and I talked to some people, all of whom said they often see shoes in the middle of the street. Mike got a tremendous picture when the wheel of a bus just caught the edge of the shoe and shot it out across the street like a marble.

I wrote the questions I had asked myself. How did it get there? Didn't someone notice when they lost their shoe? Did he have too much to drink and do one of those things we think are so brilliantly funny when we are drunk, like throwing a shoe out the window? Or two folks might have been enjoying each other in an entwined position in the back of a car or a taxi and somehow a shoe and other pieces of clothing went out the window.

I checked with the ambulance drivers, who reported there had been no accidents on that corner. And to end the story I rescued the shoe from the street, picking it up and leaving it on the sidewalk under a street sign. Actually, I was checking to see if there were any toes left inside. Whatever the reason for it being there, it was a mystery, and mysteries give life flavour, I said. But it was still just a shoe in the middle of the street.

The morning after the story aired there were scores of comments on the overnight call-in log. All of them favourable. Thank you, Mike.

Later in the day we went back and the shoe was gone and a note had been left there, thanking us for finding it. There was no name, but we got a second story out of that. Did I say, "Thank you again, Mike"?

Ten years have passed and I still hear, "That shoe in the street. Now *that* was a neat story."

If I ever become an executive of a large company and don't have someone smart like Mike Timbrell, who never finished high school, telling me what to do, don't buy shares in it. Which reminds me of another story . . .

Okay, Twist My Arm Again

Dave McKay, who is a cameraman and sings in his own blues band at night, and I had been looking for a story. We looked up. We looked down. I got out of his van and asked people if there was anything fascinating, neat or passably interesting in their lives. One after another they shook their heads and I got back in his van, banging my shin on the way. I have a row of scars on my shins from the thousands of times I have gotten back into the vans of cameramen after not finding a story. I am despondent and not very careful after a failure and *crash*, the front of my leg bangs the edge of the step.

If the story works I do not bang my shin because I am happy, and when I am happy I am alert and conscious of both the world and the hard edges of steps on vans.

So far on this day with Dave I had gotten several more bruises.

"There's something," he said, pointing to a family setting up a picnic near the road.

"No way," I said. "No way am I going to get out and ask 'Why are you having a picnic?' and be told 'Because we want to.' Then I will come back and get in your van and probably bang my shin again."

"Get out anyway and ask," he said.

"No."

It is not easy putting up with a pouting reporter, but Dave stopped his van where the sign said No Stopping, then put a tape of one of his recording sessions in the tape player and turned it up.

"I'm not moving until you ask them."

"Ask them what?"

"What the heck they are doing here," he said.

"I'm embarrassed," I said, and I meant it. There gets to be a time during the day when you cannot go up to one more stranger and say, "Hello, I don't know you but can you think of any reason why we should want desperately to put you on TV?"

They think and think and then reply, "No." Then you have to back away without hurting their feelings because they did not pass the Worthy-to-Be-on-TV Test. I truly feel sorry for some of them. I imagine them going home, afraid to tell their friends they were *almost* on TV, but their lives were too dull. It is a modern-day social plague.

"I mean it," I said, "I am *not* asking them. We will keep driving until we find something that we know will work, and we will do that."

165

"Out!"

Dave sings about rusty old pickups and broken-hearted cowboys. A voice that has character can sometimes make you do things that you have no intention of doing. It is like the purring of a woman saying, "Won't you *please*?" And so you drive two hours back where you came from because she forgot something that you know she can live without, and her voice reaches in and strokes something deeper than your ears.

Dave has a kind of roadside gravel in his voice and when you say no to that, you really have to duck.

So I got out and walked back to the picnickers. I said, "Excuse me, but is there any unusual reason you are having a picnic?" What I *heard* myself saying was, "Excuse me, but I know I look like an idiot interfering with your day and I feel foolish and if I had any talent at all I would have found a story hours ago, but please talk to me and tell me something amazing, even though I know in my heart you are just ordinary picnickers having an ordinary picnic, and I am now going to leave you and bang my shins again."

"Sure," they said. "It's amazing you picked us to talk to." They were having a picnic because it was their dog's birthday and they had brought a cake for him and they were going to light some candles on it and help him blow them out. Then they would sing happy birthday to their dog, which was right now sitting under the table with his tongue out.

"You're kidding," I said.

"No, not at all. We do it every year."

"Wait, please, wait, wait!" I shouted back at them as I ran for Dave.

I yanked open the door of his van. "Hurry. It is the greatest story you've ever heard. You won't believe it. I told you it would be great. I told you we had to stop."

Dave shot the cake and the singing and the dog wagging his tail and the dog eating the special dog bone and the people eating the cake and laughing. We finished and went back to his van.

"I don't know how you do it," Dave said. "You have an uncanny sense for finding these gems."

I opened the door and carefully climbed in.

"You name the coffee, and I'm buying," I said.

One City, Two Tales

I must tell you about one other story with Dave McKay. We were as always looking for something fascinating, uplifting, odd, happy—anything that would leave a smile at the end of the show.

We thought of measuring piles of garbage, and there were some mighty big ones growing, especially in the back alleys, because the garbage workers were on strike. We drove into a lane just a few blocks from Vancouver's Gastown where all the tourists are, but there was something else here.

There were young women. A few were standing and some were crouching behind the garbage. Most of them were in their early twenties. Some might have been in their teens. In the next alley there were more. In three lanes we saw more than a dozen of them. They were all, each of them, every single one of them, shooting heroin into their bodies, or some possibly deadly mixture of heroin and cocaine. Some were settling into a daze on the ground after the drugs started to swirl through their blood. A few had a wide-eyed look of desperation as they searched for a vein so they could push the needle into their arms or legs.

I don't know why it was all women. Maybe some pimps were distributing the drugs they use for both payment and locks and chains. Maybe it was just coincidence. It doesn't much matter. The truth and the reality is that these women didn't care that we were stopped in a van to watch them. In one alley we got out and walked. Those who were in the process of injecting looked at us with vague scorn, and then they ignored us and continued their ritual. A woman would tighten a rubber band around an arm or a leg until a vein swelled up enough to take the needle. Injecting drugs can cause the veins to collapse, and finding one that still works is sometimes tricky. Then she took the syringe and, without even wiping off the tip on her clothes, she jabbed in the needle and pushed down on the little plunger.

I have seen this many times. I have talked to men and women while they were in the process of injecting themselves. It is so common you have probably seen it on television. It is not hard for a cameraman to get an assignment to film someone shooting heroin and to come back with pictures in less than an hour. In the Main and Hastings area of Vancouver, for example, where we were, it is as easy to find someone shooting heroin as it is to find someone littering.

But what got me on this day was the number of women we saw crouched low with mountains of garbage around them while they searched for euphoria. The festering, putrid garbage was swallowing up these women, all of whom should have been in a college or office cafeteria drinking coffee and talking about problems like too much homework or computer glitches.

Once the drug was in them they were in heaven. Some leaned against the walls. Some stumbled and fell into the garbage. We could smell the stink of it. They couldn't. It hurt both our hearts so badly to see it because in a few hours those women would do anything—anything, things most of us can't imagine—to get more drugs. And there are people who will make them do those things, and do them again and again because they own the drugs and therefore they own these women's souls and bodies.

But on the other hand there is so much bad news on television that to take these pictures only makes the whole world look worse, and it doesn't change anything. It is our job, our unique job, to bring some good news to TV at least once a day. So we left the alleys and we found a little boy in Trout Lake park who was missing pre-school because he had broken his leg.

He was playing in a sandbox with his mother nearby. He had a cast on his leg. He wanted to go to school so he could learn to be a doctor and fix "owies," he said. He knew how to sing "The toe bone's connected to the foot bone . . ." He knew the whole song and he was only four years old.

It was such a pretty story and we did it and I hope it made people feel good. It did that for us. But back in the alley, only a few blocks from the police station and the tourist highlights, there are girls putting needles into their arms.

Both stories need to be told: the boy who wants to be a doctor because that gives us hope for the future, and the girls who need care and protection and a life before theirs ends on an ugly pile of garbage.

But one of those stories needs more than telling. It needs a solution, and it needs it badly. It is an emergency. The patient is dying.

Trash TV

At the end of every story, when the cameraman and the reporter part company, the cameraman gets on the radio and tells the newsroom how much tape they have shot. The practice began years ago to let the editors know the size of the problem they will be facing.

"Two tapes coming in on the mayor's race."

"A tape and a half coming on the hockey game."

Then it became a contest: can we do this on one tape, meaning we must have more pointed questions and sharper pictures? Can we keep this to fifteen minutes on a twenty-minute tape? That is the sound of a reporter and cameraman who know what they are doing.

On the other hand there are the fumbling questions and meandering pictures.

"So-and-so is on his way with three tapes."

Someone else calls in to say he has four tapes.

"Four tapes. Did you hear that?! What a boob."

That is the laughter of cameramen and reporters listening on the radios in other vans. Okay, it's not a gut-splitting Late Show joke, but when you haven't got anything of your own shot yet and the time is growing short and you know disaster and chaos, or at the very least panic, are waiting for you in the next quarter hour, it always helps to laugh at someone else.

But on one story the unbelievable happened. John Chant, cameraman, went on the air and said, "McCardell is on his way in with four minutes of tape."

"Impossible."

"No way."

"He's full of it."

Ha. In my hand was real life, real television, and considering the amount of mileage we got out of it, it stands as the most economical story ever shot in the history of BCTV news.

It started with a glance out of the side window. We were riding past the train station on Main Street in Vancouver, and John was driving. "That really ticks me off," he said.

"What?" I said. I saw nothing.

"The garbage," he said; then he added, "and I thought it was you who was supposed to see things." He pointed at a McDonald's bag on the ground. It was open and overflowing with paper and it lay next to the driver's door of a new $60,000 Audi.

"Oh," I said, being insightful.

"I wonder if it came from them," said John. He was looking at people inside the car, who were eating.

"Let's park and see," I said, making a major decision.

This is the fun and the ridiculousness of our jobs. The hair on both of our heads, what little is left of it, is going grey. We both have grown-up children. But we both get to play undercover cops. If we are right we will possibly make a score. If we are wrong we will slink away and never tell anyone that we wasted half an hour waiting to see if someone dropped some paper.

"What did you do today, Daddy?"

"Well, son, I played cops and robbers. But the criminals with the out-of-place paper napkins got away."

However, on this day we were like the Untouchables catching Al Capone red-handed with a smoking gun.

John parked a few spaces away from the Audi and the bag on the ground. He got out his camera and started taping them while we were still sitting in his van. A minute later a wad of paper napkins came flying out of the driver's window of the expensive car.

"Did they just do what we just saw them do?" I said.

"Got it right here," said John, patting his camera.

We got out of the van and walked over to the car.

"Excuse me," I said. "We are from a television station and are wondering why you threw this stuff out."

"What stuff?" said the driver.

"The stuff that you threw out of the car."

There were four of them in the car: two guys, two young women, all of them well dressed.

"I'll pick it up later," he said.

"But we want to know why you threw it out. And is this bag yours?"

I knew I was getting a bit pushy and I was hoping that he didn't know kung fu or have a baseball bat in his car and a desire to show off in front of his girlfriend.

"*Excuse* me," he said with great indignation, "but I think I have the right not to answer your questions."

"You do," I said, "but we have the right to ask them."

He started his car, and when you pay that much for your basic transportation it starts immediately. Then he stomped on the gas going backward, and again when you pay that much for a car it accelerates faster than you would believe.

No way are you getting away without cleaning up after yourselves, I thought. I grabbed the bag of garbage from the ground and in that nano-blink of a second when he went from reverse into drive, I had him in my sights. He was the enemy in the snowball fight who poked his head up. He was the fish in the lake that you have hunted for months. He was the escaping garbage-dropper who for one instant was caught between going backward and going forward and had not yet rolled up his window.

I did the only mature thing a guy in his mid-fifties could do. I got revenge. I threw the bag in through the open window. Bull's eye! It was not harmful, except maybe for the leftover greasy fries and the open ketchup packets. He was now going forward and he did zero to really fast in very little space. I managed to throw the napkins at the window as he rolled it up, but they bounced off and the litter war was over.

However, on this battlefield, John, the veteran cameraman of many real police actions, had shot everything. Without that it would be a story told to few and quickly forgotten. With his pictures I looked like Billy Bishop shooting down the parking-lot litter bombers.

We got a couple of comments from passersby and we were done. Four minutes of tape that became two and a half minutes on the air. That is unheard of in television. Mostly the ratio on TV is ten to one: ten times more is shot than makes it to air. In Hollywood it is forty to one; actors flub a lot of lines. *Sports Illustrated* photographers shoot a thousand pictures for each one that shows up in the magazine. *National Geographic* has the world record in being choosy: ten thousand to one. John's ratio was better than two to one, putting him in the ranks of the nearly unbelievable.

Then the phone calls started. Before the story was over the switchboard was flooded. "Throw those bums in jail." "That's disgusting, those litterbugs should be arrested."

There were almost four hundred phone calls that night. Usually a good reaction to a story is half a dozen calls, each one representing about a thousand people who wanted to pick up the phone but didn't. The story ran again the next day and it got two hundred more calls. They kept coming in for a week, almost all saying jail, torture and fines for the litterbugs.

But amid all the praise for me was one response from someone who saw it differently. It came in a letter telling me that the writer had seen me throwing an apple core under a bush, and therefore what right did I have to criticize others? I wrote back with my defence: it was not paper, I was feeding the birds, it was natural and would decay and add nutrition to the earth. Actually I took it as a warning. Just because you have a camera, don't think you have superiority. The undercover morality cops are everywhere. And I learned my lesson: now I eat the cores.

And while we are on the subject of saving the world, there was the case of the man who rescued the goldfish.

Go Fish

Karl Casselman, a cameraman who skis, scuba dives and runs so fast doing stories that he sweats, even in the winter—which is good because he eats two or three times more than most other human beings—and I were out hunting for a story. That sentence, like Karl, is larger than life. He finds enthusiasm for everything. We see someone changing a car tire and we decide to do a story about him. "Tighten those lugs more. Pump that jack. Let me see those hands strain." That is Karl, the director.

We see someone locked in a police paddy wagon. Karl puts his nose and camera against the window. "Who are you? What did you do?" That is Karl the reporter. The arrested, handcuffed, screaming-mad prisoner shouts back at Karl words no one should use and swears he is innocent. In a moment the police will manage to get this intruder with a camera away from the wagon, but before that happens Karl has pictures and words from someone who may be very important in a story someday.

We were not doing such dramatic things on this day. We were looking for something nice when we saw an abandoned house near China Creek Park in east Vancouver. The door was nailed shut, the first-floor windows were boarded up and the upstairs ones were broken. A neighbour told us it had been a shooting gallery, a drug hangout, and they had had a lot of trouble with the people who lived there and the police coming almost nightly. Now it sat ugly and forgotten. This was not nice, although the obituary of a house might be interesting.

We looked and poked and hunted but it was not coming together. We had never seen the house in happier days, so to do a story now would be an injustice to the good times. We were going to leave when the neighbour told us there used to be a fish pond in the backyard. Once again, story god, thank you.

He helped us lift some rotting plywood and two-by-fours and there, beneath still more garbage and some rags was a dark, water-filled hole. All I could see were some potato chip wrappers floating on top. The neighbour told us that before the druggies had moved in, the resident of the house had fed the fish every day. But that was a couple of years ago. Since then nothing had been done with it.

Karl went back to his van and came back with a studio lighting kit. He hooked up batteries and a cable, and soon we had a spotlight drilling into the murky darkness.

A minute after that, "My god, there's something in there."

It's good to state the obvious. At least you won't be wrong.

"There it is again."

A fish we could barely see slid by under a Doritos bag.

"That's amazing."

And truly it was. For at least two years it had eaten bugs and algae. That may be what fish are supposed to eat, but this one had spent the first part of its life as a pet living on predictable handouts before it was abandoned. Karl took pictures and then we left the pond as we had found it. The story showed the discovery of the house and then the fish, just as we had experienced it.

That night a viewer called the SPCA: he demanded that they go and save the fish.

"No way," said the SPCA. "The fish is not in harm's way."

So the viewer called me.

"No way," I said. "The fish is doing fine."

But he wasn't going to let "No ways" stand in *his* way. The next morning he was at the hole with a fishnet, the neighbour later told me. He scooped out the little Dorito-eating fish and took it away.

When I heard about this I thought it was a ridiculous act of self-righteousness. First, he was stealing from the owner; even if the house was abandoned it was still owned by someone. Second, there are those starving children in Asia and Africa who get ignored, while a local goldfish, which appears on television, gets attention because it has a dishevelled home. Come on, get your priorities straight.

Then I thought: What a neat guy. He saw something that he wanted to make better and he did it. He didn't think something should be done and then do nothing; he acted on what he believed. He found the house, rolled up his sleeves—literally—and rescued a fish that would never give him any affection in return. Who the heck am I to call that self-righteous or misguided?

A few weeks later I passed by the house and saw a bulldozer knocking it down. Its steel treads were rolling over the spot where the hole had been.

Thank you, sir, whoever you are.

One of my favourite stories is about people who make an unpaid career out of rescuing others. And in this case there is no story behind the story. It all happened in front of us on camera. The North Shore Mountain Rescue people, who are a heroic breed unto themselves, were going out for an anniversary dinner. These volunteers include plumbers and gardeners and doctors and nurses, all of whose personal lives are secondary to their passion for climbing mountains at night through rain and snow to rescue others. Why they do it is some mystery deep in their souls that defies understanding because they literally risk their lives and get nothing in return.

This happened on a summer afternoon in the mid-1970s. They decided their dinner would be formal, with gowns and tuxedos and candelabras and ballroom dancing. They also decided it would take place in the setting in which they felt most comfortable, on top of the tallest peak of the twin mountains called the Lions. Along with Naomi Stevens, one of a handful of women who have taken news cameras on their shoulders and outshined many guys, I got up the mountain by helicopter. Luckily, to be in the news business you only have to watch others who are heroic, you don't have to join them in their every step.

The rescue people moved up the rock of the mountain one inch at a time. On their backs they carried the tables and chairs and linen tablecloths and dishes and food and wine and stereo equipment and candelabras and candles. In their backpacks they also carried the floor-length gowns and tuxedos they would wear to dinner.

Naomi and I were there to document the event, and the fact that these people not only had the skills and strength to do it but the imagination as well made it a stunning gem of a tale. They cooked on a barbecue grill, they ate at formal place settings on a red tablecloth, and they danced on the top of the world in a ballroom with no walls. To be brave enough to rescue people at night you've got to have some wild nuttiness in you too.

But then the unplanned sparkle came on the story. Naomi leaned over the side of the cliff and saw someone climbing up this same mountain. He had his fingers in the crevices. He was sweating and breathing loudly and fighting gravity to achieve his movement of victory so that he could stand proud and alone at the top of the world. She put him in the lens of her camera and she panned back to the black-tie dancing, then moved back to the climber just as he peeked over the edge of the cliff. She filmed him as his eyes opened wide and his face filled with disbelief, and she kept filming him as he slowly lowered his head and climbed back down. We don't know what mountain climbing meant to him after that, but Naomi's picture made a lot of people laugh and feel good that night—probably the mountain climber too, and that is a great achievement.

I would like to tell you about one other rescue mission, which never got on television. I was working with Ken Oreskovich, who is now a freelance cameraman. We had covered forest fires together and were told by the firefighters that when we were out of our truck taking pictures to keep the truck facing in the opposite direction with the doors open and the motor running. We thought they were overly cautious until we saw a fire rip through a valley far below us, and then in less than a minute explode up the side of a mountain on the other side of the valley. Ken got pictures of a natural firestorm that made you stop breathing even when you watched it later on television. He looked pleased with the shot, and then we saw the fire coming up our side of the valley. The camera was thrown in the truck and we jumped in with a foot on the gas before the doors were closed. We watched the fire in our mirrors as we raced back along the logging road that had brought us in. If we had had to wait to open the doors and find the key and start the engine and turn the truck around, neither his pictures nor either of us would have made it back.

But that is not the story. Another time we had to do a simple story along the Squamish Highway when workers were blasting out the rock cliffs to make the road safer. We knew where they were working. We parked our van and loaded up our equipment and started walking past a sign that said the road was closed. We heard a whistle. "I think they are blasting somewhere near here," I said. We kept walking. Another whistle. "I hope we can get a shot of this," I said. We kept walking and saw in the distance a group of workers. They were waving. I waved back. "I'm glad they're friendly," I said. Another whistle and more waving.

"You think they are trying to tell us something?" said Ken. We were on an open stretch of road with a rock wall on one side and the water on the other. We were a hundred yards from where we had left the van and a hundred and fifty yards from where the men were still waving, but now waving more frantically.

Another whistle. "I think we have a problem," said Ken.

Then from the group of workers appeared a large front-end loader. It pulled away from them and came at us faster than I have ever seen any piece of heavy equipment move. "Oh, damn," I said. We didn't need further explanation. We turned and started running. In a minute the front-end loader slowed as it reached us and the driver shouted, "Get in," and pointed at the bucket in the front. We did, and it was caked with mud and dirt and the steel was hard and hurt my shins and the camera fell to the bottom of the bucket and the driver stepped on the gas again. He had just reached the sign that said Road Closed when a series of explosions tore open the rock wall and tons of boulders and mud and dirt came flying off the cliff and landed where we had been standing.

To the driver, I never got your name, but thanks.

There is a different kind of acknowledgement to Wayne Decoffe. He looks like a biker who forgot to eat. He is a cameraman. He is rail thin, and his arms are covered with tattoos. But never judge advice by its skin covering.

We were doing a story on my car, which I have mentioned elsewhere is old and wrinkled, and on this day it had passed what I thought was a significant milestone: the odometer read 400,000. That's good enough for me, I thought. Who could not love an aging machine? I talked about the mileage and how I had driven the Alaska Highway in it and across the country twelve times and how faithful I am with oil changes. It was a pretty good and conclusive story, I thought. Then Wayne asked how I got that dent in the door.

"My son did it, and I see it more than I see him," I said. Wayne still had the camera on during that brief exchange.

And what did people care about the next day? Was it how wonderful I was because I had kept the car going so long, or how fascinating to have taken all those trips? No, hardly a word on those. What I heard was, "that's just like my kid. Dents a fender and he disappears." There is a lesson in that both for journalism and Basic Life 101. After you brag about the big news, always mention the dents.

There is another case of the ordinary things of life bringing back memories that last generations. I was working with Mike Louie, who is a cameraman, but whose real talent is that he can make computers sit up and beg when he snaps his fingers. He is so good with them that he was hired by a dot-com company and sent around the world to write programs. Then dot-com died and now he is back with a camera.

He is a generation younger than me and grew up in Vancouver, working in his father's corner store at a time when small Chinese groceries were the only place to shop and working in them was endless back-breaking toil. But he did manage to get out at night and play street games and it turned out that they were the same games I played decades earlier in another country on another seacoast.

Kick the can was his favourite, and it was mine. And he played Johnny Ride a Pony, a game that would be frowned on now for being too rough because you pile up on the other team until they collapse under your team's weight. It was good to remember games that had no computers and required no purchases, and I talked about them to my friend Carlo the editor, who you will soon learn about, and it turned out he had played the same games on the streets of Rome. So I wrote some magazine and radio stories about them. No television. You could only imagine them, not see them. And I imagine that somewhere kids are sneaking out somewhere tonight to play Kick the Can and Johnny Ride a Pony, and someday when they are grown up they will meet an old man named Mike Louie and will be surprised to learn their childhood games had a heritage. They are like dents in a fender. When they trickle back into your memory, they tickle you and make you smile.

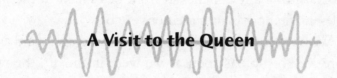

A Visit to the Queen

This story is about the glamour of reporting on royalty. It unfolded just before Expo 86 and we were off to see the Queen.

"We" were Deborra Hope, the anchor; John McCarron, the cameraman; his assistant; Dirk DeJagger, the sound man; and myself. We met on a dark, rainy, windy morning on the banks of the Fraser River near the old BC Penitentiary. We were going to fly to Victoria on a float plane. The weather that morning was very rough. Deborra wore her new dress, bought just for seeing the Queen, but she was wrapped in a big raincoat and was staring unhappily at the plane bouncing toward us on top of the water.

I did not like the thought of flying in this weather either. Nor did John. But Dirk was different. He had no fear. He was a member of a search and rescue team, and he was also a pilot. "Don't worry about the rain," he told us. He said he had flown in much worse, and this would be a snap.

We took off, we three guys squeezed into the back and Deborra sitting a few inches in front of us next to the pilot. Single-engine float planes are not very big.

We bounced off the water, and bounced again and again before we got up. As soon as we were in the air, the wind knocked us sideways and there were four passengers gripping their seats with sweaty fingers. But not Dirk. Cool as a veteran, he beamed self-confidence.

Another punch from the wind, and Deborra and John and I shrieked and groaned. But not Dirk.

Then we rose higher and the plane settled down a bit and we settled back, with our thoughts turning to how to cover the story.

A few minutes later I heard John ask, "What's wrong, Dirk?"

Dirk's face was changing colour. It was a shade of grey with tinges of green. "I think I'm going to—"

"No you're not," we said. There are no bathrooms in single-engine planes and no way to open a window.

"Yes, I am," he groaned.

The pilot shrugged in despair. He said he had none of those bags available, those bags that are used in situations like this.

He told us to take the plastic sleeves off the ends of the life vests, which we did, and we shoved one into Dirk's trembling hands. Without trying to ruin your lunch, I still have to tell you he immediately leaned forward and filled the bag.

The bag was very shallow, so he filled it to the top. Then he handed it to John, who passed it to me as Dirk filled a second bag. Dirk then gave his second steaming open plastic container to John as he reached for a third bag, which he immediately filled to the brim.

Now we were each holding one of these hot, stinking bags by our fingertips as Deborra leaned as far forward as she could without pushing her head into the dashboard. We tried biting our tongues to keep from thinking about the odour that rose from the open bags that were swinging between our knees.

Gradually the rain disappeared and the sun came out, while we prayed that what we didn't want to think about would not slip out of our fingers and fall over our shoes. Victoria appeared below us, all cleaned and polished and crowded. We kept digging our teeth into our tongues.

We glided down for a landing in the harbour, and as soon as we touched the water the doors opened on both sides of the plane and three warm plastic bags went flying out into the shimmering inner harbour. We littered, we're guilty, we apologize. Then we all went off to see the Queen.

The glamour of the job is sometimes hard to get across on television.

Strike Report

The first thing you learn about walking the line is your legs and feet are hurting, but you are not getting any exercise. This is not like walking around your neighbour-hood or walking to get your heart rate up, or walking down the street to buy a newspaper. On a picket line you spend a long time going a short distance, then you spend a longer time returning over that same path.

"What the heck are those people talking about?" you ask someone who walks past going the other way. You are referring to the negotiators.

"I don't know," is the answer as the other person turns and walks backwards. You also turn and walk backwards because you have to keep walking, but you don't want to stop talking to each other.

"I hear they broke for lunch," says the next link in the chain as she passes you.

So you turn around and walk forward again while holding up a sign that says you refuse to work. Not working has become your work and since you are not working you are not getting paid for it, which makes perfect sense, except after days that turn into weeks this gets to be harder than work, so we should be demanding a raise for not working so hard.

But to give myself a break from not working I pretended I was working and took some notes on the strike. This is what I jotted down:

While the negotiators were sitting around an oak table covered with papers, one of the pickets kept passing a pile of broken wood. He was Ryan Steeves, an editor, and each time he passed this pile he slowed down and thought about it. The wood is mostly from broken delivery skids and was being fed into a fire in an old oil drum. Picket lines always need a fire to keep the troops warm, even in summer.

Ryan stepped out of the picket line and took an axe that someone had brought to cut up the wood. The axe was half hammer and half cutting blade, and he used it to pry out and straighten some nails, and then he hammered and chopped at the firewood. He had no other tools, but in less than an hour he made a solid, strong table that the strikers could use. Without management, without a contract, without a time clock or pay envelope or deadline or work order or coffee break or two people watching while he hammered and cut, he turned some junk into a useful thing. Neither the union nor management believe that is possible.

While Ryan was building the table, Steve Lyon, a cameraman, had brought along his little daughter to the picket line. Steve is a single father. His daughter, whose name is Savannah, was almost three. She was happy being there because she met Jamie's dog. Jamie Forsythe is an editor and his dog is a miniature schnauzer. The dog had been walking back and forth and back and forth on picket line duty, probably thinking this is not fun, until Savannah got there. Then the two of them played together on the grass. Savannah called the dog Toto, which isn't his real name, but he didn't care because having someone to play with was better than walking on a picket line, especially if you have tiny schnauzer legs.

And then Linda Aylesworth and Darcy Griffith, both reporters, started throwing a child's football back and forth. But Linda throws like a girl and the ball kept going into the company parking lot where union pickets were forbidden to enter. They had to sneak across the line to get the ball. To prevent this from becoming a big issue they stopped playing and went back to walking back and forth and talking about what books they were going to read if the strike went on for a long time.

Then came the reporters from other TV stations and newspapers. It's a scary thing to face someone with a notebook and a camera. Can you trust them? You don't know them and they're asking you questions and taking pictures of you. I don't know if I like that. If I ever get the chance to work again I'm going to make sure I'm extra nice to anyone I interview.

A bunch of engineers who usually work on electronic equipment pitched in and did a smart thing. Engineers are noted for solving problems so they picked up the porta-potty and moved it out of the sun and into the shade. I think management must have shivered when they looked out the window and saw that. The resolve of the strikers became stronger.

But by then Toto and Savannah had fallen asleep under Ryan's table, and when the pickets passed them they tiptoed. There was no chanting of slogans like "less work, more pay" anywhere near the sleeping pair. There are some things more important than contracts or picket lines, and at that moment they were curled up together under a homemade table.

Country Dogs, Stray Cats and Weak Bladders

One day Sergio Magro, a young cameraman, and I were driving on back roads toward Fort Langley, BC. As always, we were looking for something that would entertain us and therefore, we hoped, entertain others.

"Wooo," Sergio said as he swerved around a brown thing with a tail lying in the road. "A country dog."

Sergio grew up in Prince Rupert. He knows about country dogs. I don't know about country dogs. Anything pausing long enough to lie down on the street where I grew up would be a squashed thing.

"They have the right of way even when they are asleep," he said.

Sergio is first-generation Canadian. His family is Italian. His parents came to Canada searching for work and found it on the railway, in Prince Rupert when there were still wooden sidewalks that got soaked in the rain. From a hot village in northern Italy to a wet, remote town in western Canada, that is one heck of a culture gap. But Sergio learned about hockey and toques and country dogs. We talked of the difference between Italy and Canada and how his parents had to use all their energy to adjust. And when we stopped talking we were in Fort Langley.

Every spot on earth has the same potential to be fascinating or boring. It is all in the beholder. On this day one of the beholders who was searching for something to behold was as blind and stupid as they come. That was me. We spent an hour driving and walking around Fort Langley, which is a beautiful town with many interesting people. But in the back of my mind was something that was preventing me from seeing anything else.

"Why didn't we stop at the country dog?" I asked.

"Because you wanted to go to Fort Langley," said Sergio.

"You think it is still there?"

"Country dogs never move," he said.

We drove in a rush to get back to the dog. Over and over I thought, how ridiculous can I get? We are hurrying to return to a dog that I am hoping is still asleep. It was sleeping an hour and a half ago.

"How long does a dog sleep?" I asked Sergio.

He looked at me as though the question didn't deserve an answer. Well, Okay, he had a point.

"As long as it wants to," he said.

I am thinking, why didn't I say when we first saw it, "that's neat, let's take a picture of it"? I didn't because I forgot my first rule of journalism. In fact, it is the first rule of avoiding all regrets in life: never, ever, pass an opportunity. Never. Don't spurn life's gifts, no matter how odd and tiny they may look. The same applies to the stock market and making friends. Don't look down at something as you pass it because you think something bigger is around the corner. Nope. Never, because running back later to try to grab what you missed makes you look as dumb as me, who is now saying, "How much farther was that dog?"

When we got there, the dog was still in the same spot. Oh, story god, thank you.

Sergio set up his tripod so he could get pictures from a distance. The dog looked beautiful. A car came along and swerved to miss him. This was heaven unfolding before the lens. I could write about the idyllic world of the country dog and how local respect for it changes traffic laws.

Then the dog got up and·shook himself.

"Oh no. Oh please no," I said. "Please, lie down."

But he didn't. He looked around, glanced at us, and slowly walked off the road.

"Come back. Please, come back," I pleaded from the edge of the universe, which is where I might as well have been.

The dog squeezed under a chain-link fence and walked to a house, which was the only one for a quarter mile and was obviously where he lived. He climbed the front steps, then plopped down in the shade on the porch.

"Oh, dog. Oh, please." I leaned over the fence and pleaded. "Come, dog. Please come." I made kissing sounds, which is the way I thought you were supposed to call a dog. I clapped. I snapped my fingers. I said the stronger version of darn.

"Country dogs are like that," said Sergio.

It raised its head. There was hope. Then it moved a paw and put its head back down.

"Nooo. Tell me you are not comfortable."

For ten minutes I tried calling, wishing and shaking a paper bag that I put pebbles into so it would think we had food. Sergio and the dog just watched me.

But we did have one picture of it sleeping and one picture of a car going around it, and those were not going to be wasted.

"Would you take some pictures of birds and anything else you can find," I asked Sergio.

He took beautiful pictures of blue birds on telephone wires, and a cat that came out of the weeds and some birds flying overhead and some wildflowers, and he took a picture of me walking down a country road while talking about the character and strength of country dogs.

"Wait. Tell me more about them," I said.

"They are independent and self-reliant and they just don't give a damn about anyone," said Sergio. "Take your case for example."

I took a breath and said in a standup, "Country dogs are independent and self-reliant and they do just what they please, whenever they please."

We drove back to the TV station, and with the help of an understanding editor we soon had a beautiful piece about a country dog that started with birds sitting on a wire, and then a cat coming out of some weeds and then a picture of the dog. Over the next minute and a half I spoke about the virtues of country dogs, and on television there was one picture of a dog, followed by pictures of birds flying overhead and a cat coming out of the weeds and wildflowers, and then a car going around the dog, followed by more birds sitting on a wire. And then there was a picture of the dog waking up, which Sergio was smart enough to shoot, and shaking the sleep out of its eyes and walking off, which is the way many stories end. It was a touching tribute to a dog, and a reminder to me to never, ever, no matter what, pass an opportunity that is sprawled out and sleeping right in your path.

Here is a good example of taking advantage of an opportunity. Ken Timbrell and I were called in a panic one day while we were looking for a story. The ICBC building in North Vancouver was being evacuated because of a bomb scare. We were requested—and turning down the request was not an option— to go there at breakneck speed. When we got there we found a group of people outside the building and the area roped off by Mounties. Ken took some pictures of the police dogs arriving and the people milling around, and I knew that was just the beginning. Bomb scares mean long waits.

There are many bomb scares. They are called in by nutcases who would find life much better if they locked themselves in a room and screamed obscenities to each other. At least they would be among people of the same IQ. Real bombings, of course, are ugly beyond description. They hurt and kill people who almost always have nothing to do with the situation. Do you take all of the calls seriously? Yes, of course. Do you downplay it so the caller thinks his threats are as unimportant as he probably is? That gets a double yes.

At the ICBC building, half an hour had gone by and nothing had gone bang. Probably nothing would happen. The people were outside, the police and their bomb-sniffing dogs were inside and our chances of getting a story that would be uplifting were slipping away. No disaster: good. No happy story: well, no one will know that the bomb scare took away the time to find another story because we will not air it, so bad.

Ken and I left the area, but we did not leave sight of it. We went to the old shipyards, one block from the bomb scare. We could still see the ICBC building. We drove by a movie set and passed some warehouses and saw a fellow standing in front of an old building that once was used to build parts of ships in. He saw me and waved. He was a welder whom I had met months earlier. We talked. He was looking for his cat.

Thank you again, story god. In half an hour we had a tale of the man who worked in an abandoned warehouse next to a dry dock, twenty thousand square feet of space, the size of two football fields, and somewhere in there was a cat. Ken was able to get wonderful pictures high up from piles of junk. He had trained as a ballet dancer for twelve years before he burned out and took up the camera. He has no trouble now jumping up on places that I would need a stepladder to get to. But we never saw the cat. We saw only the search for it, which is always better because to hope and long for something, as my mother said, is almost always better than getting it. Trying to find a cat that had been a stray and then got taken in by a kindly man and now lived in a house twice the length of a 747 hangar is better than having the cat cuddled in his arms. He was a man on a mission, to find his cat so he could feed it.

The great missions in life are never quite accomplished. If Don Quixote had slain the dragons in his mind there would be no fable. If the windmills had fallen under his lance there would be no pathos, no tragedy, no comedy. Don Quixote never conquered those dragons with the turning arms, and the cat was not found. It was a story of a search to share love. That beats a bomb scare any day.

And during it all, we were never out of sight of the ICBC building, at which nothing happened.

There is another place that is always interesting: bathrooms. During the Vancouver civic workers' strike Al Coen, a cameraman, and I were on the hunt for anything, as usual. The boss back at the TV station told me that they had heard seniors were being kept from their daily outings in community centres because of the pickets. So we went to Trout Lake park in east Vancouver, which has the smallest beach in the city at the edge of the lake in the middle of the park. It also has a community centre.

As soon as we arrived at the centre we saw a man who looked like he was in discomfort walking away from the building.

"What's wrong?" I asked.

"The bathroom is locked and behind a strike sign," he said.

Poor guy.

"It looks like we have a social catastrophe here," said Al, who along with me had to go to the toilet.

It is problems like finding a bathroom that can change the course of some of the great events of the world. If you have to go, really have to go, you can't be bothered about things like world peace or retirement investments. For a few minutes until you can find a place to go, nothing else matters. The entire universe may be heading for collision with another universe, but that is nothing compared to a full bladder. Young people do not know of this pain. If they live long enough they will.

But where do the pickets go? They are not all young. They put in four-hour shifts drinking coffee and walking back and forth and drinking more coffee and they cannot use the toilets behind their own picket lines.

"We go down to the restaurant on the corner," said one picket.

"We've made friends with some neighbours," said another.

"We suffer," said the most honest one, who had pain in his voice.

The agony of the picket line without a toilet made a story with the kind of characters many people could sympathize with, even non-union members, and as soon as we finished Al and I literally ran to the other side of the park.

Remember that smallest beach in the city? The beaches were not behind picket lines and all beaches have a changing room, with a bathroom.

If this does not sound dramatic, you are young. Someday you will understand.

Another time I had to go while we were passing Strathcona Park, just east of downtown Vancouver. Eighty years ago the area was a garbage dump. During the Depression it was a hobo camp. Now it is a soccer field next to the wholesale vegetable depots for the city's grocery stores. But the only thing that mattered to me was I had to go. So we stopped and I ran to the bathroom, but there was a rope across the door with a sign that said: No Entry. Inside two guys were painting the walls to get rid of the graffiti.

I started to plead and it felt like water was coming out of my eyes. The painter nearest the door looked at me, and without saying anything took pity and moved the rope aside. I stepped over the paint cans and did what I had to do and the world returned to normal.

"It's a good thing you looked so pained," said the other painter.

"Why?"

"Well he wouldn't have let you in if you didn't look like you were going to explode," he said, pointing to his colleague. "He's deaf."

"Really?" I asked.

"Totally," he said.

These two guys had worked together for ten years, and had become the closest of friends despite the fact they had never had a conversation that was not based on lip-reading or smiles and gestures. They worked together, drank beer together and visited at each other's homes. It was a story of patience and love and laughter and a magical deep understanding between two men.

Their story turned out beautiful on television, and I have only my bladder to thank for it.

The Silent Jitterbug

"A re they dancing without music?" said Roger Hope. He is a cameraman. He is married to Deborra Hope, the anchor. In one family, a face is in front of the camera and a face is behind it.

But that doesn't mean Roger is unknown. You have heard his voice. Every time a reporter stops the formal interview to take a breath, there is Roger, behind the camera, talking, asking very simple, obvious questions: "So tell me, why did you shoot the drug dealer?" "But suppose the economy doesn't pick up?"

The reporter is yelling inside his head, "Roger, shut up, this is my interview." But the reporter doesn't actually say anything because before he gets the words out he hears the interviewee giving his first honest answer. Roger looks friendly and unassuming, and besides, he's just an ordinary working guy behind the camera. Sure, says the drug dealer, I'll answer his questions.

But there were no questions the day we saw the silent dancers. They were on top of Queen Elizabeth Park in the middle of Vancouver, where folks gather to do Tai Chi in the morning. But this couple was dancing. Just a man and woman with no radio, no tape recorder, going from swing to bebop to waltzing.

"What are you doing?" I asked.

They were bored by Tai Chi, they said, and they like to dance. What could be simpler than to get your exercise this way?

So Roger got out his camera and began to record them, dancing silently. But that is not what went on television. Roger is also a musician, who writes music and says some day he will sell a new Broadway musical or, even better, a Coca-Cola jingle. And while Roger was filming the couple dancing, silently he started composing and it was just too much for his mouth to hold back.

He began humming, then scatting—that's those made-up jazz words that Ella Fitzgerald made a career out of—and then he slipped in some rock and roll lyrics. Well, so much for the story about the silent dancers. That was disappearing before my eyes and ears. But you know what happens when you are dancing and you hear music? The couple he was taping started to hum, then sing. Then another couple joined in.

The only one left standing was me, brooding because the original story was gone before it got into the camera. There was only one thing left for me: to burst into the opening lines of "Rock Around the Clock." One o'clock, two o'clock, three o'clock rock. . .

We were all dancing now, even Roger with his camera. No longer was this a story about people dancing for exercise. Nope, all because Roger had started humming, it had been transformed into a circus of fun and laughter, which outside of love and peace is the only truly unbeatable combination.

Things like that sometimes just happen, and they make you feel so good. The moral? Encourage your children to hum, and to ask all the questions they can.

Whose Bed Is This Anyway?
And Don't Forget to Pack the Hair Dryer

When I was new at reporting I wanted to be a foreign correspondent. First, their stories were usually short, so I could get away with doing less work. Second, they had romantic lives because they were always covering wars instead of the local parks board meeting.

Some years later I was inside a sewer in Soviet Central Asia cursing the people, cursing the assignment and telling myself that never would I go travelling again when the travelling meant hauling three hundred pounds of equipment around in addition to my underwear.

But before that, I went with a crew to the streets of Hong Kong, where life overflowed before us and some of the most incredible pictures were magically appearing everywhere. There was thick traffic and giant buildings and millions of people yelling. It looked like the street I had grown up on, except no one here was speaking Yiddish or Italian.

Grant Faint was the cameraman who had arranged the trip because he didn't really want to be a news cameraman. He wanted to be a photographer who would get paid to travel the world by himself, taking still pictures with a small camera. But first he had to get around the world to prove he could take those pictures.

I had worked with Grant a great deal in Vancouver and while we were driving to assignments he almost always pulled over to the curb in his van, took out his still camera and took pictures of mountains or flowers or trees. And then we would go on to what we were supposed to do. Every week he would take a load of slides and send them to an agency in New York that supplied stock pictures for advertisers. He sent them thousands of pictures before they started buying a few.

"Look at this," he said to me one day when we were following a politician through the streets of Vancouver. He dragged me to a newsstand and pulled out a magazine. On the back cover was an ad for a brand of cigarettes featuring a mountain scene. What cigarettes have to do with mountains is beyond any imagination.

"That's my picture," he said.

He was so proud he could burst. And he made more from that photo than from a week of carrying a thirty-pound camera on his shoulder and chasing politicians.

He eventually took every picture possible in Vancouver and he needed a wider field to work in. At the same time he learned that Cathay Pacific Airlines was opening a service from Vancouver to Hong Kong. He contacted the airline and somehow managed to get us a flight there so we could do a series of stories in exchange for mentioning that the airline was now flying there. The airline would have no editorial control at all over the content of the stories. We could show the good, the bad, the ugly or whatever we found exciting. And we would make these arrangements clear to the public so there would be no hidden agenda.

This was a good offer to the television station accountant, who rarely approved a travel budget north of Hastings Street in Vancouver. A week later Grant was looking at the teeming streets of Hong Kong and aching to get started, because once he was finished with the television work he could take pictures with his own camera and get his beloved career going.

"It's not working," he said.

"What's not working?" I said.

"The damn camera is not working," he said.

We had brought double everything in equipment— except the camera. When you pay $60,000 for a television camera it's not supposed to stop working.

"It's not working."

Ken Chu, another cameraman who grew up in Hong Kong and had come on the trip to guide us, was in a phone booth trying to find someone who could fix it, immediately.

Dave Baker, the camera assistant, was shopping for a tie. Dave was very handsome. Dave was always well dressed. Dave wanted to be a lawyer, not a camera assistant, and he was only doing this to save enough money to go to law school.

Ken came back with information: it was probably the humidity. The soggy sponge of the city's air makes the wires inside cameras sweat. That is not good for them. He had a friend who could take it apart and dry it out and we would get it back tomorrow.

"Tomorrow? We only have a week here," said Grant. "We can't afford tomorrow."

"I have a hair dryer," said Dave.

A hair dryer? Why would you carry a hair dryer on a working trip? There is so much other stuff to haul around. Reporters and camera crews usually try to get all their personal belongings into a briefcase, not a suitcase, and a hair dryer would be the last, heaviest, bulkiest thing you would want to take. But a hair dryer could fix the camera.

"Thank you, Dave."

He later did become a lawyer and is now defending criminals in Vancouver and no longer packs a hair dryer when he travels. He simply buys a new one when he arrives.

But back to the hotel room in Hong Kong with four guys trying to take apart a camera using the screwdriver of a Swiss Army knife.

"You better be careful. That part looks important."

We had pieces on chairs and on the bed and on the floor, and the hair dryer was blowing at each set of wet circuit boards, turning a disastrous one-day delay into a minor two-hour setback.

Time is the biggest problem. We worked fifteen hours

a day then viewed the tapes and made notes for two hours at night. You are only going to be in this place once, you have never seen it before and you can't go back and get more pictures and interviews later. It is not like being a tourist and taking a picture of a historic church. Here you are, plunk in the middle of the Poorman's Night Club, a seedy area where you can get dinner from a pushcart, watch a two-piece orchestra and dancer on the sidewalk and get your teeth fixed by a dentist while sitting on the curb. It is overwhelming. And we were trying to capture it all.

There were thieves who wanted to take our camera. There were pickpockets who would take what was left. And mingling with them were scary-looking people who would pick over our bones. Most of them didn't want a camera pointed in their direction. Then there was the vendor mixing a green drink in a glass that hadn't been washed since it left the factory, and Grant was saying, "Drink it. It will be a good picture." I drank it. The vendor laughed. The scary-looking people laughed. Ken Chu said, "You didn't really drink that, did you?"

We did a week's worth of stories of people living on boats and a woman raising ducks near the border with China and the Hong Kong stock market. We even did a story on the racetrack, which combines culture with gambling in a way Western tracks will never achieve. Sixty thousand people all screaming for different horses are at every race. That is like the Super Bowl every day, except the Super Bowl sometimes is boring. The track in Hong Kong, which is called Happy

Valley—which sounds more like the name of a mental hospital—is drenched in adrenalin.

My problem was that Grant and Ken had left Vancouver a few days before Dave and I, and when we flew we were put into business class. I had not yet learned that one drink of anything is quite enough for anyone. So on the sixteen-hour flight I had several drinks of free Scotch and/or champagne and/or whatever it was that they gave me. When we arrived my head felt like someone had parked a John Deere tractor on my scalp with the motor running, making the seat shake—and the plow was digging into my stomach. Plus, when we had boarded the airplane in Vancouver the temperature was a delicious fifteen degrees. When we got off it was a searing, Tabasco-like thirty-nine degrees and the humidity was just getting warmed up at one hundred percent. It felt like the John Deere's radiator had sprung a leak that was pouring over my head.

It was the last day of racing for the season. "We don't have time to go to the hotel," said Grant. "We got to get right to the track."

An hour later I was interviewing the Hong Kong railbirds, while the horses pounded by and my head screamed for quiet. Then I stood among the crowd to do a standup, which is when I am supposed to give my feelings and insight about whatever it is that we are doing.

"Oh, God," I prayed. "Just help me stay vertical for ten more seconds."

Then with a smile and a gesture to the sixty thousand, I said, "The Kentucky Derby only gets this once a year. Here it happens every afternoon, with enough money wagered to finance a small country."

"Good," said Grant.

"I think I'm going to throw up," I said.

Then I collapsed into a chair. "Please. Aspirin. And coffee. And a bed," I pleaded meekly. That part was not in the story.

The amazing thing about travelling with a camera crew was that we moved so much, slept so little and got so bleary-eyed that I really didn't see where we were until weeks later when I watched the tapes in the editing room.

Grant stayed on after we were finished with our week of work and travelled through Southeast Asia with his camera. Over the next several years he arranged other trips like that for him and me, and because of that I saw Japan and Korea.

Japan was like stepping into the next century with everything run by computers and with efficiency the only acceptable way of life. But what I remember most was sleeping in a capsule hotel. It was a warehouse full of rooms the size of large coffins stacked on top of each other. I climbed a ladder to get to my room and inside I had just enough space to sit on my bed with my head touching the ceiling. But it had a TV and radio and telephone and lamp. And it had a tiny compartment to put my socks in. The door was just a curtain, barely two feet high. But since everyone in Japan is polite there were no sounds of TVs or radios or even snoring. However, I shattered the silence when I sat up and banged my head.

Korea was fascinating because we did stories on

Canadian veterans returning to the old battlefields. We went with them to the border between the north and the south. Since the war is officially still going on, thirty thousand American soldiers are there, all with loaded guns pointed at the north.

We toured the spot at the border where tourists are allowed, and Grant started shooting the guns and the soldiers. When we got back on the bus with the old vets there was a commotion outside among the American soldiers. They surrounded the bus with their M-16s pointing at it. Several got on the bus and said we had taken pictures of unauthorized facilities. They wanted the tape.

I started arguing with them, saying we were just here with these heroic Canadians and there was nothing in our pictures that anyone couldn't see, that is if their eyes were as strong as the hundred and twenty-millimetre lens on the camera. I probably said that part less loudly than the part about the heroic Canadians.

Dave Baker, the future lawyer and the soundman on this trip, popped the tape out of the recorder and handed it to them. I was angry with him for giving in so easily. And I was angry at the US soldiers because I really believed that if they had anything that was so sensitive they would not be allowing busloads of old veterans up there. But I was most angry because a story of the Korean border without pictures of guns and soldiers would be lacking authenticity.

We drove away and I was despondent. I glared at Dave. Then he reached down under his seat and pulled out a tape.

"I hope they don't have a machine up here that plays that format," he said.

I tilted my head in a question, too stupid to realize what he was saying.

"I switched the tapes, you idiot," he said.

"Oh, Dave. You're going to be a good lawyer." Then I prayed the bus driver would not slow down.

I worried about that tape until three days later, when we were in the air heading back to Vancouver. The pictures were beautiful and powerful. The story was about the vets visiting the graves of their fallen friends and touring the border. There was also the time we were on a dusty road and I was interviewing an old Korean farmer. He had lived in a hole in the ground for two weeks with his family, surviving by eating roots and drinking rainwater while soldiers fought on the ground overhead. In the middle of the interview we were pushed aside as an armoured column of South Korean troops went by. It was a dramatic and scary moment that taught many viewers about the ugliness of the past and the unpredictability of the present.

When you add to that interview the pictures of the guns and soldiers at the border you've got an idea of how long the bitterness of war can stick in the throat of a country.

After the work in Korea, Grant took off again with his own camera, shooting and sending slides to New York. A few years later the New York agency hired him. He left BCTV and spent the next decade travelling the world, carrying only a few small cameras, going wherever he wanted to go and taking pictures of whatever he liked. His photos were used as

the background of hundreds and later thousands of adver-
tisements in magazines around the world.

There were two benefits to his new life. First, he didn't
have to put up with reporters. Second, he was paid well
enough so that he is now retired and happily living on
Vancouver Island. He is ten years younger than I am, and an
inspiration.

What I learned from working with Grant: do what you want
to do. You will at the very least amaze your friends, and you
might even do the same for yourself.

A Lodging for the Night

When you travel you must spend at least some time sleeping. And when reporters travel they hope for first-class beds, or at the very least, clean sheets.

Cameraman Eric Cable and I did a story near Whistler, BC, one weekend before Whistler became an expensive, tourist-filled sushi town. Back then it only had a few cabins and no tourists, and no place to stay. Those travelling through the area stayed at Bralorne. That was a town of loggers and women strong enough to push them around. It was not hard to find the hotel in Bralorne because it was the only building that had HOTEL painted two storeys high on one of its walls. It didn't have a name because there were no other hotels in Bralorne

"There's two of you?" said the man who owned the hotel and who was also the day clerk and the night clerk.

I nodded.

"Pity," said the man. "I only have one room and one bed."

It was just as advertised: a single room with a single bed for a single person. There is no point in complaining when there is no one to listen to your complaints, so we took the mattress off the bed and put it on the floor and planned to lie with the top half of our bodies on the mattress and our legs on the floor.

Eric is a large man and very strong. He plays rugby when he is not chasing politicians with his camera. Next to him I never look like I need to go on a diet. We lay down back to back and, without taking off any clothes except our shoes, we fell asleep.

And that would have been the end of the story. In fact there would be no story, except that in the middle of the night a key turned in the door.

I am a light sleeper. I opened my eyes just as the lock started sliding. I was not concerned because having Eric next to you is like having a loaded gun, if you can wake him up.

The door opened and there stood a man in cowboy hat and cowboy boots. "This is my room," he said.

"No it's not," I said, but it didn't much matter what I said because the man with the cowboy boots and cowboy hat got down and squeezed in between us.

Eric grunted and moved over. My giant protector had his personal safety catch on. I thought, what the heck, this will build character. Our visitor had a cigarette behind his ear and his breath smelled of the one he had just smoked. I turned over to put my back to him.

I really would not have minded sharing a single bed with two other guys if our new guest hadn't started dreaming. He must have been dreaming of his girlfriend because he moved closer and closer to me. This is not character building, I thought, as I pulled myself out of his embrace and rolled off the mattress.

I crawled over to a corner of the room and got an Agatha Christie novel out of my bag and sat on the floor reading under a lamp on the table. The man with the cowboy boots continued his dream, but this time he snuggled close to Eric, who does not like being the object of another man's dream. He woke up, shook the confusion out of his eyes and looked at me. Then he turned his head and looked at the man who was falling in love with the back of his jeans.

It is hard to describe the look on Eric's face at that moment, but in the next moment he got up and put one hand around our guest's collar and the other around the back of his belt. He then picked the sleeping man up out of his dream and, while I held the door open, carried him out to the hallway and dropped him.

If Eric drops you somewhere you really do not come back and dispute the issue. Mike Tyson might, but not many others.

Eric and I resumed our half-mattress sleep until sunrise. Then we went to the café and found our visitor sleeping very uncomfortably on top of a table, using a sugar shaker turned on its side as a pillow. As it turned out, the poor fellow was a truck driver who often stopped in Bralorne—and always used that room.

We woke him and bought him breakfast. I bet when he got home he had quite a story to tell, about the guys who broke into his room and how, single-handedly, he threw them out. It's doubtful, though, that he told his girlfriend about his dream.

If the Sex Is Boring, This Must Be Amsterdam

A few years later I went to Amsterdam. And everything would have been fine except the producers back at the television station wanted to squeeze as much work as possible out of this trip.

A group of us were there because it was two years before Expo 86 and someone in Holland had discovered that Captain George Vancouver was actually a Dutchman.

"Okay," I said, not wanting to jeopardize the possibility of getting a trip out of this discovery, "I'll agree with anything."

We might think George Vancouver was English. George Vancouver himself might have thought he was English. But according to the Chamber of Commerce of Holland, his family was actually Dutch, and perhaps Vancouverites would go to Holland to seek the family tree of the man for whom their city was named.

"Okay," I said, sure that this bubble was going to burst, but still hoping to get a trip out of it.

I am pretty sure it was the Dutch tourism department that paid for us to go. I am not absolutely sure, because I was afraid to ask, because then we might have a conflict of interest and how could I do an independent story?

But then came those conniving producers at BCTV, who at that time were airing a show featuring local entertainers. We had already been given two seats by the Dutch tourism people, one for the cameraman, Don Timbrell, and one for me. But the producers got two more free seats. These were for a country and western singer and her guitar-playing accompanist.

"What does this have to do with Captain Vancouver?" I asked.

"Nothing, but would you just shoot them with some windmills in the background," said the producers. "We are looking for the Dutch country music effect." He actually sounded like he knew what he was talking about. Hence, when you hear producers speaking, don't trust them.

Three days later the singer, guitar player, cameraman and reporter were in Amsterdam in an ugly, dark tent sitting on a long board held up by cinder blocks. We were watching a sex show put on by the two most bored people who have ever had intercourse on this planet. It is hard to explain how coitus can make you yawn. Even his penis was tired. I was not aware that an erection could point downwards. But we were in Amsterdam so we had to see a sex show; that is an unwritten rule.

The next day we went to the town where George Vancouver's ancestors supposedly came from before they moved to England. His family came from nobility, our hosts said. His roots went back to a castle, which the town had just restored and which was open for tourists. And, in an amazing coincidence, we were there on the same day as the ribbon cutting was held for the grand opening of the castle.

A scaled-down model of that castle was constructed in front of the Four Seasons Hotel during Expo 86, and later it was bought by Bill Vander Zalm, who later became more famous in British Columbia than George Vancouver. He put the castle into his Fantasy Gardens tourist development. It was all simply a business deal, except if you go to that castle you may hear the ghost of Captain Vancouver walking the hallways and saying, "How can you doubt a story that is so faaantastic?"

We did a story on the castle in Holland and a few other touristy things around Amsterdam. But then, despite a very tight schedule, we stumbled on a barge hauling bicycles out of a canal. It turned out that bike theft is rampant there and after the thieves get to where they are going, they throw the bikes into the nearest waterway so they don't get caught with the stolen goods. We spent half an hour doing that piece. After we got back and BCTV ran the stories on the castle and Captain Vancouver and the tourist spots, we got one comment: "That was a neat story about the stolen bikes."

There are two outstanding memories I have of that trip. One: on a cold, windy, rainy day we went out in the country near a windmill. It was the only day the producers had worked into our schedule for the singer. In front of the windmill she sang about cowboys and horses, and the guitar player played with rain running off his nose. Windmills had nothing to do with the words and the rain had nothing to do with the music. The segment never aired. Moral: don't trust producers.

And two: Just because we were in Amsterdam, Don Timbrell had to go to the red light district. He said it would be a cultural experience. I went along just for the walk, and on that walk I saw many women leaning out of windows with red lights behind them. What you saw was what you got. Or at least what Don got. But the part that made it memorable was that he got it inside a church, which I think may have lost some of its sanctity as a result.

I waited outside. Honest.

On walking back to the hotel room I said, "Well?"

Don said, "Not bad." But he added that the Canadian dollar didn't go as far as he thought it would.

We flew back to Vancouver and the only question anyone asked was: "Did you go to a sex show?"

"Yep."

"How was it?"

"Boring."

"Really?"

"Yep."

"Bummer."

The Sistine Chapel of the World

The most beautiful place on earth, better even than a nudist beach, better than the Rockies or the New York skyline or Paris by night, is anywhere in the Yukon. It is the only place I have seen where nature says to mankind, "You may think you're strong, but I'm in charge." Nature in the Yukon has a gutsy personality.

The first time I saw its low-rolling hills, its tundra, its bareness, I felt a sense of belonging. I can't explain it. I don't want to explain it. I love the Yukon. Seven trips later the magic is still there.

It was the mid-'70s and I met a man whose name I have forgotten. But I remember his hat. It was a beaten-up, black felt cowboy hat and pinned to it were gold nuggets.

"It's worth about $30,000," he said.

He was from Quebec. I remember that about him, and that he was a news cameraman in Montreal working for the

CBC when he saw a documentary about the Yukon. He quit his job and moved.

"I would not have a hat like this in Montreal," he said.

And there was the man who wore a freshly ironed and starched shirt and a string tie. He did not look like a gold miner. But he pulled from a pocket in his creased pants a nugget the size of a Zippo lighter.

"It's worth about $10,000," he said.

"You carry it with you?" I asked with absolute astounded wonder and memories of New York. "Aren't you afraid someone is going to steal it?"

He looked around in the vast openness. You could see the horizon from any direction.

"Where would they go?" he replied.

That is why I like the Yukon. Because people don't go to steal. They go to be free to struggle. They go to give the earth what they can of themselves and the earth sometimes gives them back little trinkets. People who choose that kind of life are wonderful, no matter who or what they are.

On the way to the Yukon we stopped at Mile 150 on the Alaska Highway. There was a gas station with no name, and a café next to it that had a sign reading Café. The man pumping gas was short and squat and looked like he had the muscle of a pack of bulldogs. He was from Texas and had decided to move north one day.

When he crossed the border, he said, the Canadian immigration people asked him what he would do. "I have a chainsaw and a pickup truck," he told them. "I'll do whatever I have to." He and his wife and kids built the gas station and the café, and when it burned down they built it again.

Inside the café there were truckers and miners sitting in hard, wooden booths, smoking, drinking coffee and eating bacon and eggs. But in one of the booths you could hear, "The cat walked over the grass. The little girl said, 'Hi, cat.'" It was school, taught by the wife of the bulldog. She had been a teacher in Texas and now she was teaching her grandchildren in a place that had no schools.

Those kids are grown up now. I don't know who they are or what they are doing, but if you ever run into someone who is proud and full of courage and resourceful, ask them where they went to school. They might say in a café at Mile 150 on the Alaska Highway.

Where's My Hot Water Bottle?

A year later I was sleeping on the ground in a teepee fifty miles east of Carcross in the Yukon in the winter. I was inside a sleeping bag that had to be pried open because it was frozen. I was wearing my boots and wool socks, and long johns under my pants. I also wore two undershirts, two shirts on top of those, a sweater on top of those and a borrowed heavy parka. I had a beard and around that I had wrapped a wool scarf that covered everything except my eyes. On the top of my head was a wool toque.

I looked up through the opening at the top of the teepee. Even the stars looked like ice, and quite honestly, I thought I would die.

The top of the tent was open to let the smoke out because there was supposed to be a fire in the centre of the floor. But neither Max Lindenthaler, the camera assistant, nor I could get the fire going. He turned out to be a very good photographer and I can type pretty well. While those may be useful talents, neither of us could make a fire.

We were in the Yukon again because some tourist group had sent press releases about how Whitehorse was growing. An editor at the TV station read them and told us to go and see.

When we arrived the tourist group suggested we start by visiting the mayor, and then take a tour with some officials from the Chamber of Commerce. We were in a coffee shop while they were talking to us. They were wearing suits and carried briefcases. But off at a side table, sitting by himself drinking a cup of steaming black coffee, was a man in buck-skins and a coonskin cap. He had a pack by his side. After the tourist people finished their briefing and left, we almost knocked a chair over getting to the man in buckskins.

His name was Dick Person and he lived in a teepee with his wife. He taught wilderness survival. Yes, we could visit and do a story. Yes, the story god lives in the Yukon.

Several hours later we met him in Carcross, a town south of Whitehorse. In a diner there were a couple of talking parrots, which we would have done a story about if outside wasn't standing the man in the coonskin cap, with his pack on a sled and a dog ready to pull it. A sled dog beats parrots any day. We rented a couple of skidoos on which our equipment and our bodies sat. Then while we drove across a frozen lake half the size of Rhode Island, we watched Dick run. He didn't want to tire his dog by riding on the sled, so he ran alongside.

Almost an hour later on the other side of the lake we reached two teepees, about twenty feet high. Dick had made them out of sailcloth. Outside it was thirty-five below, inside the first thing I saw was his wife Jean, wearing just a shirt and pants and washing her hair. She poured rinse water over her head and the water went onto the floor, which was made of pine boughs. This was just like I had read about once in a book on how the Indians lived.

But most of all I felt the warmth inside the tent. It was toasty warm. In a few minutes we were out of our coats and hats and were sitting on furs that were spread over boxes in which all their belongings were kept. Hanging from the sides of the teepee were crayon drawings made by their grandchildren, who lived with them during the summer.

They played guitar and sang and Bill Szczur, the cameraman, took pictures. We had coffee and ice cream, which they kept in their thousand-square-mile freezer outside the tent.

Then came bedtime and Dick told us we could use his guest teepee. It had a place for a fire in the middle and extra sleeping bags. Dick put his foot into one and cracked it open. Max and I thought it would be a hoot to sleep there. Bill was thinking of a hotel in Whitehorse.

"You're crazy," we said.

But he went, and while he was going across the lake on the skidoo, Max and I tried to get a fire going. While Bill was still on the lake Max and I gave up the fire and got into the sleeping bags. While Bill was starting our rented jeep in Carcross, Max and I were wrapping wool scarves around our faces. While Bill was driving to Whitehorse, my scarf was coming loose and my cheeks were freezing solid and I was waking up in pain. When Bill was getting into a warm bed in the hotel, I was looking at the stars through the hole in the teepee and quite honestly, as I said before, I thought I was going to die.

Morning came about three months later. Time does not fly when you are shivering through the night. We fought to get out of our sleeping bags, which had frozen hard on the outside. But then we had a most incredible experience. We walked to the lake and as the day warmed slightly—meaning it rose from forty below to thirty-five below zero—Max and I heard a lightning-fast thunderbolt shooting across the ice. In the Air Force I had heard the sound barrier cracked. This was a crack that kept moving.

It was the ice splitting and groaning under the changing temperature. It happens every morning, like an alarm clock that you don't ignore.

Dick stepped out of his cozy tent, casually putting on a coat. After one look at us he said, "You would have been more comfortable if you had lit a fire."

He invited us in for breakfast. Behind the tent, hanging from a tripod, was the frozen carcass of a bear. They said they hated to kill anything, but twice a year they killed animals, and that was all the meat they needed. We had bear steak fried in a cast-iron frying pan. There are only about ten meals in my life I will remember until I die. That is number one.

Bill returned much later in the morning and saw our bleary eyes and said we were nuts to stay the night. Wrong.

We did the story and interviewed the couple and

brought the tape back to Whitehorse, where the tourist folks were impatiently waiting. No, that is not true. They were furious because the mayor had been kept waiting. We apologized and went along with them and saw the new and improved Whitehorse.

The stories about Whitehorse ran and were forgotten. The story about the couple in the teepee travelled around the world. Various news agencies buy and sell stories from each other. The teepee story ran in Australia, England, the US and on both the Canadian and American armed forces networks.

If you go to the Yukon and see someone putting up a teepee, ask where they got the idea. Also ask if they have matches.

Go Ahead, Ruin His Day

Just one more story from the North, about the ultimate best shot ever taken.

Don Timbrell and I were covering a dogsled race along the Alaska Highway near Fort Nelson, BC. Fort Nelson is the coldest place I have ever been, even colder than the Yukon. On a bright, sunny day it is colder than the inside of a teepee at night. That was the first time I had seen car and truck engines running all night while parked outside a motel. Pyramids of soot grew below the tail pipes.

Breathing through your mouth would sear your lungs. A scarf over your nose only reduced the pain. Plus, I did not have the right kind of boots for this assignment. There are so many things they should teach in journalism school, like put on warm boots if you are going to a cold place.

We followed the dogs along the historic highway, which up there looks like a quiet, two-lane country road.

"This is no good," said Don, who was the chief camera-man. When he said something was no good that meant we had to fix it. "We have to go into the bush. I need that great shot," he said. .

So we drove ahead of the race, then got out of the car and, through snow higher than our knees, we carried the tri-pod and camera and extra batteries and tape. It was a long walk before Don said this was the spot. He knew his spots. It was near a bend in the trail and it had a great background of hills and trees. It was banked so the sleds would tilt as they passed him.

He set up the tripod and camera and checked and rechecked the shot. It was not a big race. There were only about ten teams and they would all pass this spot almost one on top of the other. "This is going to make the story," he said. From here he could get churning feet, the steam of the tongues and the glare of the eyes of the huskies. He could also get wide and medium shots.

"Perfect," he pronounced.

My job was simple: Go around the bend and tell him when the dogs were coming. I stood in the cold out of sight of Don. There were no dogs in view. I shivered. My feet were in pain. My back was cold. My fingers were cold. But my feet—oh, they were really cold.

I could not get them warm by walking because they hurt too much to move. I sat down and took off one boot so I could hold my toes. Oh, my golly. When I got my sock off it was a scary sight. The toes were turning purple. I tried to squeeze them and then I heard a faint yelp from the dogs.

Damn. This was not a good position to be in.

I pulled my sock back on and got snow inside it. The yelping was getting closer. I got my boot on. I can't fail Don now. Come on feet, we'll fix you later, I hope. I pushed through the snow, and turned to hear the dogs getting closer, then I backed up around a tree.

"Noooooo!!!!"

I recognized that sound. It was definitely Don's voice. What was he doing here when I thought he was farther away?

If he was farther away I would not now be tripping over his tripod. I can recall it all in slow motion, his camera falling into the snow, his face with a look of disapproval. And I remember the dogs, one on top of another in the fiercest part of the race, flying past us. One, two, three, four. The camera was still under the snow. Don tried to get it up, but it was attached to the tripod and he had no way to dig it out, clean it off and focus before the dog teams ran by.

I don't remember what he said after that. Later he told me he had heard the dogs coming and the camera was already running. But he could not finish the sentence.

We got back to the car and I apologized and took off my boots and apologized and rubbed my toes, and apologized and thought of how the old miners handled this. If their toes went black, they cut them off. Then they put them in a bottle of whisky and had a sourtoe drink. They still did that in a saloon in Whitehorse.

I tried to talk about that but Don had another story. He told me that in the old days, if someone backed into someone else when he had just found gold in his pan and if he knocked the pan over and the gold fell back in the creek, then more than just the toes were cut off.

We still had a story on the dog race. It was still good. But Don raised his sons telling them a bedtime story about the great shot that almost was and the klutzy reporter who made it disappear. Both his sons became cameramen, and both his sons have told me if we ever do a dogsled race, they would appreciate it if I waited in the car.

Why Are We Here?

Five years later I was in Siberia with one of Don's sons, Mike Timbrell. Don probably would have gone except he had a liver transplant, which slowed him down. The transplant had nothing to do with his half hour in the church in Amsterdam. He got hepatitis in Mexico, and almost died. So he got a new liver, gave up the big camera and re-established a love of horse racing. He can read a scratch sheet like a novel and I think he makes more money following the ponies than he did with sled dogs.

Mike and I, along with twenty-two kids from Maple Ridge, were in a bus at the Russian border at ten p.m. This was before the Berlin Wall came down and when Russian hostility and suspicion were still solidly in place. Hollywood could not stage this better. There were guard towers, searchlights and barriers guarded by soldiers with submachine guns. We were in a bus filled with ten- and eleven- and twelve-year-olds.

The kids were on an exchange visit organized by Dave Rempel, a school principal. His plan was to take the kids to a city in Siberia where intellectuals lived, and then visit a town in Soviet Central Asia that had nothing but a coal mine.

"Why are we going there? I mean the second place?" I asked Rempel.

"The experience," he said. "It will be great for the kids. They will grow. They will mature. They will develop."

I learned that if you ask Dave Rempel one thing, he will answer you with everything.

BCTV was going along because Rempel had talked to the president of the TV station and told them what a wonderful series this would make about children meeting children. Also they could get us cheap airfare.

At the border we were taken off the bus and told to unload all our luggage. Our camera equipment weighed close to three hundred pounds and was stored in large, bulky metal cases.

"Take it off," we were told. "Open it up."

The bus was strip-searched. They looked in the engine, through the luggage, inside the luggage compartment. Then the bus was driven over an open pit and soldiers inspected the underside.

I had thought they just tried to stop people from getting out.

Much has changed in Russia since then. Capitalism is king. Nikita Khrushchev's son has moved to America and become a US citizen. And crime has taken over Moscow. You know capitalism is working when that happens.

For the Canadian kids, Siberia was a breeze. It was no longer a place of exile. The countryside was lush and the city we went to, Novosibirsk, was a showpiece. The Russians spoke English, and the families the children were staying with were given extra rations.

We did not know that stockpiles of the bubonic plague were being produced in that city for use in chemical warfare. That was ten years after Russia had signed a treaty banning it. That news came from the head of the Russian chemical warfare division, who had defected to the West and was now making a living writing books about how Russia was going to win the next war by making the rest of the world sick to death.

We toured parks with statues of Lenin and were told by many Russian schoolchildren that *Lenin* is the first word they learn. We saw plays put on by Russian kids, and each play was about Russian soldiers being victorious in World War II.

We saw many old soldiers who still wore their medals on their jackets, decades after their uniforms had been eaten by moths. And we heard repeatedly how everyone had been brought up to believe that America, with the help of Canada and Britain and France and Germany, was on the brink of launching unprovoked missiles that would destroy the Soviet Union.

I was raised the same way, except in reverse. It was not a good way to run the world.

Mike and I got into trouble only once, when we slipped

away from the tour group and taped some men and women fighting on the street. There were about fifty of them and they were holding large cans and plastic jugs. Everywhere we had seen lineups for everything from bread to socks, but we had never seen fighting before. Then it became obvious what had caused their anxiety. They were trying to get beer and they were having fist fights and ripping each other's shirts to get to the dispenser before it ran out.

All the while we were shooting we could see someone watching us. We noticed him whenever the camera came out, but this time while we were taping the fighting he stood staring at us, his hands in his pockets, not trying to hide.

That evening we were visited by an official from the tour group who was clearly angry. We were forbidden to leave the tour again, and if we did there would be consequences. "This is not the way to instill trust between our countries," we were told.

It was a difficult position. We were there to do stories about the kids' visit. But around us was an empire on the brink of chaos that few outsiders had seen, and that was part of the visit too. But if we did that, it would cut off our coverage of the tour.

Luckily for us, and unluckily for the kids, we did not have to make the choice. The next day we were on an Aeroflot plane heading for Karaganda.

Aeroflot was a distinctive airline. The inside of the plane had been painted with a brush. Some of the seats were broken and ahead of me there were three Russian travellers, but only two seats. This would be an experience.

Karaganda does not look like Maple Ridge. It is in western Kazakstan, close to Afghanistan. It is dusty and flat. If you had a car, which you would not have if you lived here, and got into it and drove until the tires wore out, you would still be nowhere closer to anywhere. But it does have coal under the dust. And to get it out, Stalin sent many of the people he did not like to this place. He told them to dig for coal or die. It was an instant town made of buildings of crumbling mortar. Outside of the few schoolteachers and the ever-present government administrators, there were no other jobs except digging.

"Again, tell me why are we here?" I asked Dave Rempel.

"Great experience," he said. "We will get to see the soul of the country. We will see another side to life. The children will remember this."

The school they were visiting had been built for one thousand kids. It had three thousand, who went in shifts from seven a.m. until seven p.m. Few children or adults spoke English. The only English teacher in the school had never spoken to anyone who actually spoke English. She had learned the language from audio tapes.

None of the schoolkids living there had ever seen anyone from the outside world. The town never had tourists; not one, ever. The only visitors before us were mining engineers.

The kids scrubbed their school for the Canadians. They swept the dirt field that surrounded it and learned to sing "O Canada." And they made Canadian flags. But they had never seen a Canadian flag. It had been described to them, so the

241

Maple Leaf was down at the bottom. The Canadian kids got off their bus gripping their luggage for protection. The Russians crowded around them as though they were rock stars or Martians. There were no stores, no shopping, no playgrounds. There were no covers over the manholes in the streets.

The mothers who went—Ruth Olde, Bonnie Willis and Lynn Thomas—should have gotten a hero-of-Canada award. They went from family to family putting warmth and laughter into bleak surroundings. The scene was always the same, the big Cossack-looking parents, the tiny apartments and the terrified Canadian children who wanted to be anywhere but here. The mothers consoled the kids, helped with the cooking even though there was little food and no spices to flavour it with, and overcame the language wall with a lot of laughter, and a little vodka. Without them the trip would have collapsed in shambles.

I was the suspicious American. I grew up in the 1950s diving under my desk in school, in practice for the atomic bomb attack by Russia.

Here in the heartland of the Soviet Union I climbed down into an open manhole to see what the sewers looked like. There was nothing down there. It did not go anywhere. There was no sewer system. It just gave the appearance from above that something worked below.

I started talking to myself; no one could hear me. I cursed Russia, I cursed BCTV for sending us. I cursed the food, which was almost always cucumbers and black bread. I cursed Aeroflot, the organizers of the trip, the dirt, the lack of deodorant, the toilets that are flushed twice a year, and the eyes that were always watching us. I even cursed the one chicken that the host family I was staying with was given for the visit, because the poor woman had not had a chicken before and she stuck it in the tiny freezer of her refrigerator without wrapping it in anything and when she tried to get it out, half of it ripped off and stayed glued to the ice. Poor woman. Poor chicken. Poor me. I cursed the injustices of the world and the phoniness and hypocrisy of the politicians who tell us lies.

As I stuck my head out of the manhole I saw Mike Timbrell pointing his camera at me. Often for interviews I carried a wireless radio microphone hooked to my shirt. Often I forgot I had it on. He had recorded every utterance, every curse.

I have been accused of doing it on purpose. Maybe, maybe not. But that one piece of unedited tape ran for years after that during the annual blooper party at the station, and each time the usual drunken audience got quiet, and then applauded. Applause by your peers is not quite as good as sex, but it can make you swell up.

One night before we left that dusty coal town, Dave Rempel asked me if I wanted to go for a ride with him. No camera. He had hired a car and driver, I don't know where he got it from, and we went far out on a dirt road with no lights and no other traffic. I knew Dave's family came from Russia, he had told us that. But I didn't know that some distant relative was living in abject poverty near Karaganda. This was a poverty endlessly deep because there was no possible way in that world to change it. And there was someone connected with the relative who was crippled. She was one of those whom Stalin had exiled to this barren fortress. Rempel was on his way to deliver some money that would do amazing things to help.

In the Soviet Union, at least in the '60s and through the '90s, if you were crippled, your life was over. There were no wheelchairs that worked, no handicapped entrances, no accommodations for those who could not accommodate themselves.

We stopped at a small, dark house on a dark road. Rempel was gone only a few minutes to deliver the money that could not be sent any other way. I stayed in the car: a stranger in the house would be frightening, he said. And then we left.

Did we come all this way to help someone? I did not ask. But I suspect those Canadian kids who learned about black bread and toilets that did not work did a wonderful thing, they just didn't know it.

When we left Russia I had six letters taped to my body under my shirt. The only way anyone had even a remote dream of getting out was to be invited by someone from another country. But all mail leaving the Soviet Union was examined and so there was no hope that anyone could write to an uncle in Montreal and ask for an invitation. One of the letters I carried was from the son of a Communist Party member we stayed with, who always talked to us of the glories of Communism. Before we left he called me aside and asked if I could take the letter with me. He handed me an envelope and said, "Please, don't let anyone find it."

I mailed them in Vancouver. I do not know if any resulted in anything. But I do know that over the next decade, Dave Rempel organized an adoption program that saved scores of babies from lives in Russian orphanages. Those children and their new Canadian parents meet once a year at his home for a big party. He gets nothing from it. If the children were not here they would have little in their lives but poverty and probably crime—definitely not much love. Because of Dave they may not have fame or wealth, but at least they will be held and kissed.

It was a good trip.

And would I go on another television excursion? Not on your life. I watch travelogues now and think that between each of those pretty shots are piles of equipment. Now I travel with a disposable cardboard camera and a big, relieved smile.

The Dark Hallway

You are a young reporter rushing back to the TV station
with a hot story. You may be just out of reporting school,
but this time you are going to show them. You have it right.
You know you do. You have all the interviews and the notes
scribbled in your official reporter's notebook. You know
what the story is about. This time the editors aren't going to
call you a mindless boob.

There is a hallway in the back of the newsroom. It is
dark. It is lined with rooms that have dark glass doors. The
shadowy figures sitting in the dark are editors.

"I'm not afraid, I'm not," you, the young reporter, say to
yourself.

"You can start editing right away," you are told.

"Okay, but first I have to get coffee, and pee, and make
some phone calls, and maybe read the newspaper and call my
mother for help."

246

Every day for every reporter begins with the hunting down of the story, and there is the working with the cameraman to figure out whether you both have at least vaguely the same idea of what the story is about. And there are the coffee breaks and the frustration when the most important person in the story refuses to talk with you. And there is the rain and there is the arguing with the assignment editor over what he or she thinks the story is about compared to how you see it. Then there is the hunt for the bathroom because you have had too much coffee and then the drive back to the station with your tape, when you try not to speed but you have to go fast because time is running out.

But that is nothing compared to walking into the edit room. That is the fire pit, the testing ground for your story. It is where veteran reporters who get lazy get shot down and where young reporters learn a great deal.

Waiting in there is the man or woman who will look at the tape and say, "What the hell do you expect to do with this? You're lucky to get ten seconds out of it."

"But it's a good story," you protest. "It's about corruption and scandal and about how things should be."

"It's not on the tape," says the editor.

"What am I going to do?" you say. You are a young reporter who got A's in school and did long stories with lots of interviews about saving the world.

"Make it short," says the editor.

In this hallway are the least-seen and least-understood people in television. They spend most of their working lives in the dark, much of it alone, looking at television screens—

except that they control what appears on the screen. It is an awesome power. In television, it is perhaps the ultimate power. They decide whether the picture of the pain of the accident victim starts here, where it is almost hard to watch but it might, just might, scare someone else away from racing on the street—or do they start the picture later, when the camera is farther away and there will be fewer complaints because viewers' dinners will not be upset?

They ask questions: Why are we showing this at all? To make a point? To attract viewers? To turn viewers off? Or just to record that it happened and move on without comment? My God, isn't someone in pain worth more than three seconds on a wide shot? So many questions, so little time.

"Quick, give me that tape of the accident! It's on the air in two minutes."

Decisions that would be argued for days in a court are made as fast as breathing, and as often.

The editors see a wink, or the tapping of a finger, something the cameraman did not notice and the reporter did not know existed, and they turn that into a moment the audience will remember. They are magicians who can take twenty minutes of disjointed tape with stumbling questions and fragments of hastily caught dramatic action and pull out of it ninety seconds that make everyone look professional. And then they put those pictures together in a story with pacing and rhythm and a beginning, middle and end, and they do it while someone is yelling in the hallway, "Hurry up, we need that tape!"

They also do it while another TV monitor in the room

is showing war movies or cartoons with the sound turned off. Their work is so intense that, to keep themselves balanced, they add more television.

Carlo Sgaetti is watching a tape backwards at high speed. By the time the twenty minutes of raw tape is rewound three minutes from now, he will know what the opening picture is and what order the rest of the scenes go in. He will also have figured out a way to condemn you for not getting more interesting pictures and for wasting too much time interviewing.

"This is impossible to fix, but I will try," he says as his fingers weave together pictures that now are so smooth that it looks as though there were three cameras shooting the footage.

Carlo is from Rome. He is machismo in a worn leather jacket and cowboy boots. He breathes passion into everything. "The button on this edit machine. If you treat it gently, like a woman, the pictures will smile at you."

But holding a paper cup of coffee from the cafeteria: "This is impossible to drink! It is *imitation coffee.*" He dreams of a sip of espresso next to the Fountain of Trevi, where he went diving for coins as a child.

He speaks better English than most professors. But at a meeting of the entire station he will stand up and say to the president, "I don't understand your language as well as you, but speaking as a humble foreigner I think your policy is f***ingly impossible to comprehend."

He will then spend ten minutes shredding everything management has spent the last three months planning and he will sit down to applause, from the president. That is the sway editors have.

Carlo once said to me that his son called one of his friends crazy. "That's not right," he said. "We should do something about that. We should teach him crazy is a hard thing to be."

Because of that I spent the next two years of my life dealing with the mentally ill and the homeless. Because Carlo wanted to teach his son about the meaning of a word, cameraman Paul Rowan and Carlo and I spent a week inside Riverview Mental Hospital. We were in the padded cells, and the locked rooms of those whose lives are so eternally hopeless that they will try to throw themselves out of any window that is open.

Paul was the perfect cameraman for shooting this story. He is a curious mixture of a man who wishes to be a Buddhist who believes in not hurting anything, while having a closet full of black belts in martial arts. He has very hard fists that pound into concrete for training. He is one of the toughest people I know, but he won't hit a fly. He seemed to understand the conflicts inside the heads of many of the people he was taking pictures of.

We met the patients who shuffle around the manicured hospital grounds smoking one cigarette after another because they say there is nothing else for them to do. I met a woman who wore a hockey helmet because she would bang her head when she heard voices. Her name was Ruth and she was very sweet and we spent a long time sitting on a bench talking.

"I have seen the outside and I sometimes wish I was there," she said. "But sometimes they act so strange they scare me." She took a long time between sentences. But there is no need to rush unless someone is behind you pushing or you are trying to get ahead of someone else. She did not have those problems. "In here, everyone acts so strange it all seems normal. You never know," she said. "You just never know."

There was something in the way she said "you never know" about anything, that sounded so wise and understanding. You never know what is going to happen or why the world is so bizarre and inexplicable or why bad things happen to those who don't deserve it—and happen with no prompting and for no apparent reason. You just never know, so you just try to get through it.

I started saying that and, by God, that woman with thick glasses and a helmet, who walked the grounds with nowhere to go, taught me something about not blaming, not cursing, not fretting, and keeping my blood pressure down. Why do crazy things happen without any sane reason? You never know.

There was one unforgettable place in Riverview. It was the room where they wait to die. It is filled with soft music and against the walls are beds with pink and blue blankets. In the beds are little old people who have been here a long, long time. One came in 1944 as a young mother who had trouble coping with her baby. Many young mothers have trouble coping, but this woman lived in an age when mental illness could describe a wide range of problems. And it could be used as an easy disposal system for people with problems.

She pressed her fingertips together as she lay in the bed staring at a wall with pictures of her family, who had grown up without her. There were photos of smiling faces and crayon drawings by grandchildren whom she did not know, and who did not know her. She lies there, day after day and year after year, staring at the pictures.

The nurses who care for the people in that room have more love and dedication than you have ever seen at a wedding altar or in a maternity ward. As we left, a nurse kissed this little old lady on the cheek and ran her fingers through her thin white hair.

"Good night, my darling," she said, and then turned out the light.

No, it is not good to call someone crazy.

We did this series in 1989, the same year that Riverview, along with all mental hospitals in Canada, were changing their philosophy. They were acting like corporations and downsizing. They were stuffing pills into the pockets of schizophrenics and letting them go out in the world.

"We have no right to keep them locked up," said the hospital administrators, and they were right.

"We will build care facilities for them in the communities," said the government, and they lied.

Over the next ten years the patient population of Riverview fell from three thousand to three hundred. Allowing schizophrenics to enter the world is a noble gesture, if only you could remind them to take their medicine. But you know how hard it is to remember your own vitamin pills? It is much harder when you have voices screaming in your head, voices that tell you many things, but none of them are reminders to take your medication.

And so some of them forget, and the voices get louder, and the people who now have freedom from the control of nurses and doctors, grab hold of their heads to drive away the voices. That makes them look strange, and when someone looks strange in a public place it is not like looking strange on the grounds of a mental hospital. Out in public others avoid them. Then some of them wander into the bad streets of the city and they bump into people who have little understanding and less humanity and they get dragged into alleys and beaten and their pockets are ripped open and what little money they have is gone.

Then these people who had been used to the quiet grounds of Riverview are left lost and hurt in parts of town where police walk only in pairs. If they steal something, they wind up in jail. If they don't steal, they wind up in food lines. In either case, before 1989 there were virtually no homeless people in Vancouver. Now there are thousands.

"Well, let's go after the government," said Carlo. Editors are never satisfied.

The series on the mental hospital at Riverview took two weeks to do. The work that we did on the mentally ill living on Skid Road went on for two years. In more than one hundred stories, we put on the TV scenes of former patients of Riverview living in back alleys and worn-out rooms of stinking, noisy hotels. Such a room has enough space for one bed with unchanged sheets, a chair and a dresser with broken drawers. It is just a little larger than a jail cell, but without the safety or free food of a jail.

We talked to hundreds of dedicated people working to make the lives of the homeless more bearable, but in every story every one of these care workers said the same thing: the floodgates of Riverview were opened, but the facilities made by the government to care for them were inadequate. It was like putting plastic pails under a hydro dam and expecting the ground not to get wet.

For me, because Carlo wanted to teach his son about the pain of craziness, I met men and women and boys and girls who have scars from their wrists to their armpits from attempts to kill themselves. Those who know about such things say if the scars are horizontal, it is just an attempt to be noticed. They will not die from such a cut. If the scars are vertical, they actually did mean to get rid of the pain in their lives and were saved by someone who had a different idea. In either case, I saw many arms completely covered with scars from razor blades.

As I got to know more of the former patients, my pager started going off more often, usually on my way home from work. Someone was sitting on a fire escape and wanted to talk to me before they jumped. I made U-turns and climbed out on the metal gratings outside their windows on the sides of the old hotels, usually to be told they really just wanted someone to talk to but they could not get attention any other way.

And the net result of all those stories? The government insisted there was no problem. Sometimes you just can't win.

But it wasn't all a waste. Carlo's son now corrects other kids about the word "crazy," and tells them about the hard facts of life of those whom others dismiss simply because they are different.

Where were we? We were walking down that dark hallway before we got sidetracked. Let us continue . . .

"I can't do it. I can't say *anything* in four seconds."

That's you, the poor young reporter, with your prize-winning story of corruption and scandal.

"This is *insane*," you say loudly enough to fill the hallway. "This is *crazy*. I've *got* to have more time."

"You've got to have more pictures," says the editor, "and if you really try, you can say memorable things in four seconds."

This is the legacy of Cameron Bell, the news director who built the foundations of BCTV. He had a bushy beard and his shirttail was often outside his belt, but he saw news like a film director creating a movie. "You should be able to tell the story without words," he would lecture and bellow and repeat like a mantra.

In the mid-1970s he did something other stations in Canada could scarcely believe. He told the editors that they were in charge and if the reporters got annoying, to throw them out of the room.

Then he scratched his beard and said to the editors, "Make the pictures shout."

In other TV newsrooms, the reporters write the scripts and the editors are slaves to what is written. The editors find pictures to match the word, which is called wallpapering over the script. As a result, the pictures look as flat as wall-paper. Cameron Bell freed the editors. They are in charge. They decide what pictures will be used. And they choose the length of the pictures. "Don't argue with me. Two seconds longer is *boring!*" The reporters then write the script to fit the pictures.

"I can't," you plead.

"Sure you can," says the editor. "Tell me some secret about what happened, the story behind the picture, and you'll have no problem."

"I don't know anything else."

"Well, then we have a problem."

Let us continue down the hallway.

"Whoops—*duck!*"

Zap! A paper dart flies across the hallway and embeds itself in a hanging Styrofoam doll that has a sign around its neck that reads "Management."

"I didn't do it," says Karl Avefjall, who is still officially in the Swedish army and is holding a plastic tube that looks like it could be used as a blowgun.

Karl loves war movies and watches them continuously on one of his TVs. He never turns on the sound, because it would interfere with his editing, and besides, he knows the plots of all of the movies. He also knows every battle of World War I and World War II, and just about any other war you can name.

Besides the army, which he went back to Sweden to join, Karl has had only two jobs in his life. He grew up in the basement of the police station cleaning off tables in the cafeteria, which his mother ran. Through elementary school and high school he worked there far out of the sunlight and surrounded by guns and strong people.

One day he asked Alyn Edwards, who was then a reporter at BCTV who covered crime, if he could get a job in television. Alyn is the same guy who brought me to the station, proving at least to me that he has a good eye for talent. But a few years later, under different owners and a different CEO, he and others lost their jobs during some corporate cost-cutting madness. Even exciting, personality-driven TV stations can sometimes act like constipated accounting companies. But before that, when Karl asked him about the job, Alyn said sure, he would take him to the station. Karl walked down the hallway and saw people making a living without cleaning tables; all they did was stick pictures together. He liked that, so he stayed. He hung around so long learning to edit by watching others and playing with the machines that management eventually assumed he worked there. They started giving him jobs to do. Karl is now a senior editor, without having gone to school or having worked in any other TV station. But one thing he definitely did *not* do, he says as he rolls up another piece of paper, is shoot that dart.

Walk down the hallway a little farther. Quick: duck again. A mini-football is skimming overhead near the ceiling. Sometimes editors step out of their rooms to relieve the tension.

Enter David Ingram's room. David comes from Ireland and loves three things: Guinness, photography and Irish music. He did not need philosophy or meditation to find the path to perfect happiness. He goes to Irish bars that serve Guinness and have Irish musicians, and he writes reviews of their music and photographs them for Irish newspapers, which in turn pays for his Guinness. That is sheer genius. At home he has two refrigerators, one for food, the other for Guinness. On the walls of his edit room is an evolving photo gallery of Irish musicians, pretty girls and Guinness beer. You could never imagine how many ways a bottle of beer can be photographed, lovingly and idyllically, until you see his collection of For the Love of Guinness.

Walk farther down the hallway.

"Which dress should I wear?" That is André Poitras. By day he is an editor with short white hair and broad shoulders. By night he is a drag queen. To be an editor means in some way or other you will be different than most others you will ever meet. When André goes to a party he is no longer André the Editor. He is Cleopatra or Tina Turner. His hair flows over his shoulders and his dresses, designed and sewn by himself, are exquisitely amazing.

But he was not wearing a dress at a recent BCTV Christmas party. He came in a suit. On his arm was a woman with silken hair and a thin soft dress that hid little. When they walked into the crowded banquet room a hush spread like a wave from the entrance until it reached the head table with the then president, Art Reitmeyer.

"Wow," he said to one of the multiple vice presidents. I know he said that because he told me. Then he said. "Is she? No, she can't be."

André's date, Bibi, was possibly the most beautiful

woman in a room filled with hundreds of beautiful women. But she, of course, was not a she. Bibi was a he somewhere under that dress, which made him or her more intriguing than anything that would be served on the dinner plate that night.

They sat at a table along with Carlo and me and our wives. Also at that table was Karen Deeney, who is the chief editor. She was there with her boyfriend who, someday we hope, will ask her to get married. He is Darrel, a career soldier, a combat soldier who served two tours of duty in Bosnia. That night he wore his formal army tuxedo with a rich, startlingly royal red jacket. You know anyone wearing something like that can stare at an enemy's gun without flinching.

Across the table from one another sat the soldier who lives in a man's world, and a boy in a dress with carefully pencilled eyebrows. After they were introduced and after they learned more about each other they did what would have made a beautiful story if I had been working that night. They reached across the table and toasted each other a good Christmas.

Now come back to the hallway and walk a little farther. A groan is coming from Carlo's room. "Damn. Yuck. I hate this. I can't do it."

That is me, trying to write the last line of a story. The last line contains the most important words in a story and for the one-thousandth consecutive time, I am stuck on what to say.

"Say the cat was searching for love, that's why he got lost in the tree," says Carlo, who is editing the story with me about a dumb cat stuck in a tree and all the kids trying to get it down.

"Say he won't come down until he smells Guinness in his water dish." That is David shouting across the hallway from his room.

Karl sticks his head into the room. He has heard the need for a line and has left his own work. "Say he wanted a good observation post so he could spy on the rats."

I try to think, but I realize their jokes have more imagination than anything I am trying to say. I am being literal, trying to say something about a cat in a tree. They are being funny, talking about the whole human-animal condition of life, the universe, and everything.

I write: "He will probably stay up there until he is tempted down by warm milk, warm arms or a warm purr." I would not have thought of that if it weren't for them.

Like many good editors, these people are far better writers than most writers in television. They live by describing what pictures mean rather than what is simply in the pictures. Sadly you don't often hear that from professionally polished reporters. In most stories you see a picture of a car skidding on ice, and you hear "Icy streets had cars skidding on them." Reporters write that and editors groan.

"Why don't you say something like," says the editor without even furrowing his brow, "cars slid like hockey pucks."

I ask why they are not writers.

"We don't need to be," says Karl. "We don't have a problem with our egos."

It is imagination and resourcefulness that drive them. They work only with what they have and can't order out for more pictures or interviews. I was stuck one day without a camera. It was after three in the afternoon and I met Jamie Forsythe, who operates one of the microwave vans. That is a camper van turned into a mobile edit suite for use on the road and for transmitting live events like sports and breaking news. It gets him and the others who run these trucks out of the office and at the scene of what is big for the day, even if it's just a weather forecast. It also can be deadly. One day Geoff Fisher was raising the antenna mast above the roof of the van to transmit a story back to the office. The mast touched an overhead high-voltage wire. Geoff was killed.

Virtually every person in television and radio in Vancouver was at his funeral. They overflowed the church and spread out onto the sidewalk. At work they compete, but when one was killed in the course of competition everyone showed up to say they were together in their sorrow.

Now, on another day a year later, Jamie was working in the same van that Geoff had been killed in. Time doesn't let you forget, but it eases the pain. Geoff was unforgettable, but this van was just a hunk of steel and plastic, and now, sitting at the controls, Jamie was having a petty problem of mine dumped in his lap.

"I haven't got a camera," I told him. In three hours the show would be on the air and I was still waiting for an available cameraman. Meanwhile I had nothing. No idea of what to do, no place to do it and no one to do it with.

"So let's fix it," he said. He suggested I find tourists with video cameras and see what they had shot.

Of course, why didn't I think of that?

That was the idea of someone who simply doesn't give up. He could have said the heck with them, if they are not giving you the tools to do your work, don't do any. He had nothing to gain from his idea, but editors just like taking what is around them and remaking it.

I grabbed some tourists and asked them to come to the TV van. Jamie hooked up some connections, even holding two wires together because the van had no patch cords that would go into an amateur camcorder. And presto, we had copies of the most jerky views of Vancouver and swish pans of people slurping back noodles in Chinese restaurants with the heads half cut off. I interviewed the camera owners with their own cameras and in twenty minutes we had a fresh, funny story. Editors are amazing.

Before we leave the back hallway there are a few others I would like to introduce you to. They will stick their heads out as we pass by. They are characters you could find in few novels, even by the most bizarre writers.

Chris Koster has his motorcycle parked outside. He goes from extreme confinement while working to extreme freedom outside of work. And while he works he watches music videos without the sound.

Mark Cameron has a battered pickup truck to take him home to his endless renovations and his new son. Oh, by the way, did he mention that his son, Sam, learned a new word today? And will someday be the brightest person in the world? Mark is like most editors: he sees potential every-where. A reporter walks into his room and hears, "Let's be daring and start the story backwards."

Monte Burt is in a hurry. He is always in a hurry. He is listening to a young reporter putting together a sentence loaded with clichés. "You can do better," says Monte. "No, I like this," says the young reporter, who is thinking, What does this guy, who is always in a hurry, know about writing? Monte does not tell him he has written episodes of *Alfred Hitchcock Presents* and *The Twilight Zone*.

Simon Boniface is listening to a reporter who has writ-ten, "He was a dead ringer" for someone else.

"Do you know what that means?" Simon asks.

The reporter looks at him in disbelief. "I don't have time for this," he says. "Everyone says 'dead ringer'."

"But do you know why?" asks Simon. He wants the reporter to know what the heck he is talking about. Simon collects words and phrases. He has a treasury stacked high and deep inside his skull of the meanings of idioms and clichés. To these he gives new life.

The reporter actually doesn't care. He looks at the clock. In five minutes his story is supposed to be on the air and he is desperate to get some words stuck to the tape before the producer runs into the edit room and shouts: "Well? Are you ready?"

While the reporter is writing Simon tells him about the small graveyards of old England, where they would run out of space. "So they would dig up coffins and take the bones to a house and reuse the grave," says Simon.

The reporter is still trying to write his story, but Simon goes on. "Occasionally they would find scratch marks on the inside of a coffin and realize they had been burying people alive."

The reporter has stopped writing. This is a better story than what he is putting on the air.

"So they started tying a string to the wrist of the deceased and leading it through a hole in the coffin and up through the ground and tied the end to a bell. That was where the graveyard shift came from." Simon knows his words. "And if someone on the graveyard shift heard the bell ring, they would dig."

"So if you saw someone who looked like someone else who was dead," adds the reporter, who has just clued into the meaning of his cliché, "he would be a dead ringer of that person. That's neat."

And that is the best way to teach things. Simon should have been a teacher. Instead he is an editor and now he is saying to the reporter, "You have one minute left. You better not waste any more time."

Across the hall John Pippus is studying Spanish. At fifty and with a grown family he has started university. "Who knows how many years I have left," he said. "I always wanted a degree and I'm going to get one." His textbooks on Latin America and political science lay alongside videotapes of world news. He reads what happened in the past and edits stories of what's happening now. In short, he is writing advanced chapters in his textbooks and with that much work and insight he is racking up straight A's in school.

He also went to Guatemala for two weeks to live with a local family and learn Spanish. When he came back he talked about the culture and the family he stayed with, but one day fifteen minutes before the show started at six p.m. and we were still editing, he said, "I learned the salsa there too." Really, I said. "Yep, really." He pushed the pause button on our story and said, "You put this foot here and then step forward and then back and then forward." He started humming a salsa tune and dancing in his edit room, but in his mind he was back on a dirt dance floor in Central America. He said being Canadian and happily married he dared touch his dance partner only by putting his hand on the small of her back, but the instructor came along and said, "No, that is not salsa." He said it in Spanish so it still counted as an educational trip. The instructor moved John's hand down to the bum of the girl. "That is salsa," he said. John stopped his solo dancing, smiled, sat down and went back to editing. To be a good editor you have to be free, even inside a small room.

There are others who have saved me by eliminating stupid questions and boring pictures. Each is strange in some way, but each can spot a good picture in a jumble of tape: Ron Tupper, who wears tie-dyed shirts and open-toed sandals; Ted Anhorn, who, when he gets stuck on how to edit something, looks at the watercolour pictures by his kids that cover his walls and then goes on with the story; and Chris Hawkes, Ryan Steeves, Murray Crooks, Jacquie McIndoe and Jean Baillargeon, who wants to be a pilot, and Russell Stephens, who trains for marathons by running to work from downtown Vancouver to Burnaby, and after twenty years in the business still gets so excited when he sees a picture he likes on the tape that he stops working and drags another editor into his room and says, "Look, just look at the feeling in that picture," to which the other editor says, "You're out of your mind." And Jim Helgason, who raises fish in his edit room and Steve Bucek, an audio editor who once kept a tarantula in his room. To each, thank you. And to John Kerrigan and Keiron Duncan, who are training to be editors, and the others who are waiting to train, Josh, Agasel and Gianluca, none of whom were born before I first walked into the television station: Do you really want to spend the rest of your lives in a dark room arguing over the inflection of a word or the length of a picture, and get as a reward the back of someone running off to take the praise for themselves? You have to be tough to be an editor, and it is a guarantee you will turn out as strange as those people you see now living in those dark rooms. Of course, on the other hand you not only get to watch a lot of television, you can also make it do what you want.

At the end of the hallway is an office less than one step wide and half a step long. It holds one chair wedged against the walls. Marco den Ouden sits there with his legs folded under himself like Buddha. He is reading a book on libertarianism. For the twenty-five years I have known him he has always read books on libertarianism. He believes in free will and free thoughts, although he does not have enough room to swing his legs under his chair. In front of him is a wall of monitors connected to the giant satellite dishes outside, and on the screens are riots in the Middle East and shootings in

Africa. Everything he sees is live, it is happening right then. Nothing is on tape. It is Marco's job to pull in from the feeds around the world whatever is needed in the current local show that is on the air. In front of him is the world. On his lap are the words of freedom. But in the irony of all life, he does not have room to slide his chair forward or back.

Back to Carlo. After the series on Riverview he began to volunteer at the hospital. He surrounded himself with the insane, cooking hot dogs for people who didn't have much else in their lives and making friends with people who stop in the middle of a conversation, shove their fingers into their ears and spin around, then return to the conversation, hardly dropping a word.

One day Carlo invited me to a baseball game. The inmates of the Forensic Unit were playing the ordinary schizophrenic patients. That meant at-bat was a murderer who had burned several people to death. Pitching was someone who heard voices. On first was a woman suffering the kind of depression that left her with scars from her wrists to her armpits.

I was at second with the team from up the hill at Riverview, where they are allowed to walk the grounds. Carlo was on the team where the players are kept behind barbed wire.

Some of the pitches were high. Some rolled on the ground. Some balls were hit. Some players ran without bothering to hit the ball.

At third, on the Forensic team, was a big man with an evil-looking face. He simply stood in front of the plate and allowed no one to cross it, so my team never was able to score a run.

I have sat in the press box at Yankee Stadium and have watched games in Shea Stadium. But that slugfest between the schizophrenics and the forensics was the best baseball I have ever seen. And we never did a story about it.

The Last Page

I was lucky to get this kind of work, nothing else, just lucky. Plus I really wanted it.

I am lucky because it has let me meet huge numbers of wonderful and unforgettable people. They are all in my head and my heart and memory and every one of them makes me feel good. People I don't like I don't think about.

But you don't need to have my job to find good people. They are everywhere. That's where I find them. Just walk down the street and if you see someone cutting the grass or shovelling the snow, say hello. That's all I do.

You don't need a camera or a slot on a television show to ask someone how they are and what they are doing. And you never know—you just never know—what stories and friendships and adventures that can lead to.

It was an amazing thing to learn that every one of us is the story god.